The
Polish
Texans

T. Lindsay Baker

The University of Texas
Institute of Texan Cultures
San Antonio
1982

THE TEXIANS AND THE TEXANS

A series dealing with the many kinds of people who have contributed to the history and heritage of Texas.

Now in print:

Pamphlet Series — *The Indian Texans, The Norwegian Texans, The Mexican Texans,* (in English), *Los Tejanos Mexicanos* (in Spanish), *The Spanish Texans, The Polish Texans, The Greek Texans, The Jewish Texans, The Syrian and Lebanese Texans, The Afro-American Texans, The Belgian Texans, The Swiss Texans, The Czech Texans, The French Texans, The Italian Texans, The Chinese Texans* and *The Anglo-American Texans.*

Book Series — *The Irish Texans, The Danish Texans, The German Texans* and *The Polish Texans*

The Polish Texans

Copyright 1982
The University of Texas Institute of Texan Cultures — San Antonio

Jack R. Maguire, Executive Director
Pat Maguire, Director of Publications and Programs

Production Staff: Sandra Brown, Illustrator; Sandra Carr; David Haynes; Meredith Rees; Alice Sackett, Indexer; and Tom Shelton

Library of Congress Number 82-82513
International Standard Book Numbers
Hardbound 0-933164-98-X
Softbound 0-933164-99-8

First Edition

This publication was made possible, in part, by grants from the Institute of Texan Cultures Associates, the Texas Folklife Festival and the Houston Endowment, Inc.

Printed in the United States of America

The Polish Texans

T. Lindsay Baker

Contents

The Poles in the Early History
of Texas

Poland, one of the oldest countries of central Europe, came into being as a separate entity in A.D. 966. In this year King Mieszko I accepted Christianity and founded Poland as a Christian state. For many years it was one of the largest and most important countries in Europe.

Poland was not without its difficulties. Probably the greatest of these problems was that the nobles assumed more and more of the power which was needed by the king during the 1600's and 1700's, when new and powerful nations were arising in Europe. This had the effect of dividing the country's power. By the end of the 1700's, about the same time that the United States was winning its independence, Poland was cut apart and annexed by her strong neighbors: Austria, Prussia, and Russia. By 1795 the Polish state disappeared from the maps of Europe, and for a century and a half no separate Poland existed except in the hearts and minds of her people. Three unsuccessful insurrections were raised by Poles—one in the 1790's, others in 1830 and 1863—but they were crushed. Only the end of the First World War and the major political changes which followed it allowed the return of a Polish state.

Most of the Poles who came to Texas did so during the many years that their homeland was divided and ruled by others. Because of the oppression that they felt, many of these people came to the New World for political freedom as well as economic and social advancement.

Partitioned Poland, after 1795

Today the Poles are by no means the largest ethnic group in Texas, but there are thousands of Texans who trace their roots back to Poland. In the first half of the 1800's considerable numbers of individual Poles came to Texas. Some of them were adventurers, only seeking their fortunes, while others came to stay and establish permanent homes. These Poles played an active role in the Texas War of Independence, fighting both at Goliad and San Jacinto. Then in the 1850's permanent Polish colonies were established in the San Antonio area by farmers from the region of Upper Silesia, in southwestern Poland today. Landing in Galveston in 1854, they traveled northwest. Settling at Panna Maria, Bandera, and San Antonio, these people founded the earliest Polish colonies, the first Polish churches, and the first Polish school in America.

The farmers from Upper Silesia were followed, after the Civil War, by Polish emigrants from all parts of their divided motherland. Most of these later arrivals settled in the lower Brazos River valley, where they became successful cotton farmers and where many of their descendants live today. Even now the Poles remain quite visible with numerous religious and secular celebrations observed in different parts of the state, and they contribute an important element to the varied culture of Texas.

The first plan to bring Polish settlers to Texas was a failure. The reason was that people in America were simply not well enough informed about conditions in Europe. In 1812, while Texas still belonged to Spain and while Spain was fighting Napoleon in Europe, the Spanish consul at New Orleans pointed out to his superiors that there were large numbers of Poles fighting in Napoleon's army in Spain. The consul, Diego Morfi, believed that many of these soldiers would grasp any chance to desert Napoleon if they were offered land in Texas

2

and transportation. Morfi maintained that the Poles would devote themselves to farming and would contribute to the welfare and prosperity of the province. He proposed to give the Polish exiles land along the Gulf of Mexico near the Louisiana border, offer them self-government, and exempt them from taxes.

The problem with Morfi's plan was that his ideas were based on his assumption that the Poles were fighting for Napoleon only because they were compelled to do so. He was wrong. They supported Emperor Napoleon as the only power on earth that could restore their unhappy country to its former freedom. Morfi's superiors, however, knew more about the situation in Europe and rejected the plan. They further stated that they were afraid that settlements of foreigners, especially former soldiers, would be dangerous in Texas, and added that they were reluctant to spend the money to execute the plan. Therefore, Morfi's idea was never realized, but surprisingly, Poles appeared in Texas only half a dozen years later.

Napoleon's defeat caused his soldiers to scatter in all directions, and many of them sought their fortunes in the New World. One group of these exiles formed an association at Philadelphia for the establishment of their own colony in America. Their goals were mainly political, with plans for the rescue of Napoleon from the island of St. Helena in the South Atlantic and for the placing of Joseph

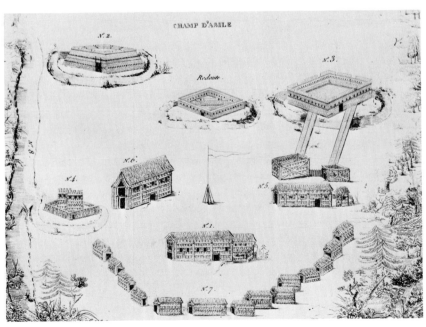

Plan of Champ d'Asile, a French colony near the Texas coast

3

Bonaparte on the throne of Mexico as the King of Spain and the Indies. The exiles established a colony at Demopolis, Alabama, but the settlement soon failed. Then in 1817 another group of veterans organized a new association in Philadelphia, this time to establish a colony in Spanish Texas near the Louisiana border. They expected to find local support for their political ventures. Early in 1818 some 400 armed men landed on the Texas Gulf Coast. The Frenchmen and Poles had been joined by other exiles: Spaniards, Americans, and former pirates from a host of nations. This group seized land on the Trinity River near present-day Liberty and formed the military colony of Champ d'Asile.

One of the participants in both of these exile colonies was Constantin Paul Malczewski, a former Polish officer in the French army and brother of a well-known Polish poet, Anthony Malczewski. When the new expedition was forming in 1817 to come to Texas, Malczewski deserted the Alabama settlement to join in starting the new one. He was one of four artillery officers who directed the construction of the fortification which protected the new settlement.

The founding of Champ d'Asile, 1818

Life in Champ d'Asile was organized on a strictly military basis, and its inhabitants were divided into three "cohorts." Naturally, the Spanish government was suspicious of this effort and sent a military force from San Antonio to oust the exiles. But sickness, hunger, and misfortune had already discouraged the colony. Many colonists took a boat to Galveston Island, were given a ship by Jean Laffite, and sailed to New Orleans. Malczewski went to Louisiana and then to Mexico. As late as the 1830's he was serving as a general in the Mexican army.

Another Pole appeared in Texas in 1821, Captain Joseph Alexander Czycerzyn. He was one of the 52 men who sailed with Captain James Long on his second expedition to Texas in an attempt to wrest control of the province from Spain. The party seized the town of Goliad and the nearby presidio of La Bahía and held them for a few days. Then a larger force of Mexican troops arrived and forced the invaders to surrender on October 9, 1821.

While a handful of Polish immigrants may have settled in Texas during the years of early Anglo-American settlement, it is definitely known that numbers of Poles came to the area after the outbreak of the Texas Revolution of 1835. Several Poles fought under Colonel James Fannin at Goliad in March 1836. Recalling the Battle of Coleto Creek, after which the Mexicans forced the Texans to surrender, one of the Texan survivors remarked that the Texan artillery officers were "tall fine-looking Poles." These officers intentionally allowed the Mexican soldiers to draw comparatively near to the Texan troops before they opened fire, whereupon they "poured shot upon our hasty and over confident assailants." Among the men with Fannin was Michael Dembinski, an exile from the unsuccessful Polish insurrection of 1830. After the Texan troops under Fannin, including the Poles, were forced to surrender, they were held prisoners for about two and one-half weeks at the old La Bahía presidio. Then on Palm Sunday, March 27, 1836, they were marched out in several groups to be executed by firing squads. Only a few escaped to tell the tale.

Several Poles participated on the Texan side at the Battle of San Jacinto, at which Texas won its independence. The best known of these men was Felix Wardzinski, who had been born in Poland in 1801 and had come to Texas in January 1836 to enlist in the Texan army. He was described by Captain Robert Oliver as being five feet seven and one-half inches tall, of light complexion with blue eyes and brown hair, and by occupation a professional soldier. After the close of the war Wardzinski was awarded a headright certificate

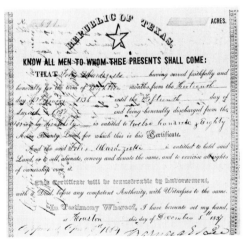

Wardzinski bounty land certificate

for one-third league of land in return for his services to the Republic of Texas.

Another Pole who participated in the Battle of San Jacinto was Frederick Lemsky. As one of the musicians, he played "Come to the Bower" on the fife as the Texan army crossed the prairie to attack the Mexican camp.

5

"Surrender of Santa Anna," by W.H. Huddle

During the days of the Republic of Texas it was William H. Sandusky in 1839 who surveyed and made the maps for Austin, the new capital. He was a descendant of Antoni Sandusky, a Pole who had come to the British colonies in North America at the time of Queen Anne's reign in England. After surveying and mapping the new capital city Sandusky served for a while as the private secretary to President Mirabeau B. Lamar and then accepted a mission as draftsman for the preparation of maps of the harbor at Galveston. Sandusky died in 1846, but in his short 33 years he made a lasting contribution to Texas.

"Austin about 1840," watercolor by William Sandusky

After Texas entered the Union in 1845 Poles continued to come as individual immigrants. One such person was Charles Radziminski, a lieutenant in the United States army during the Mexican War. After the conflict he became the secretary of the commission appointed to survey the international boundary between Mexico and the United States. In this capacity he crossed thousands of miles of the Southwest on foot and on horseback during the three-year survey. He died near Fort Belknap, Texas, on September 18, 1858.

One more Pole who came to Texas during the period of early statehood was Erasmus Andrew Florian, who became known in Texas as a banker and insurance agent. Florian, whose original name was Florian Liskowacki, was another exile from the unsuccessful Polish insurrection of 1830. Taken prisoner by the Austrians after the failure of the insurrection in Russian Poland, he was imprisoned for a number of months and then deported to the United States by the Austrian government in 1834. He spent his first two years in America working for a New York bank, then moved to Memphis, Tennessee. In 1853 he came to Texas. Within only a few years he became one of the most influential bankers in San Antonio, served the city during the Civil War as a member of the city

Erasmus A. Florian

council, was one of the first insurance agents in the San Antonio area, and helped form the San Antonio Gas Company.

The last thatch-roofed cottage in Płużnica, Poland

8

Founding the First
Polish Colonies in America

The history of the Poles in Texas changed drastically on December 3, 1854. On this day a party of about 150 Polish farmers disembarked from the sailing ship, *Weser,* at the old wooden Merchant's Wharf at the port of Galveston. These peasants, from the region of Upper Silesia, now in southwestern Poland, were to establish the first permanent Polish settlements in the United States.

In the 1850's Upper Silesia constituted the southeastern tip of the Kingdom of Prussia. The region had been cut off from the Polish state for almost five centuries when the Texas emigrants departed. Despite the long rule by foreign kings and nobles, the Polish peasants who inhabited the area retained their Polish national identity, Polish culture, and Catholic religion.

A number of factors caused the Upper Silesian farmers to seek a new home in another part of the world. Most of the causes were economic; others were social. Upper Silesia had severe economic problems during the 1850's, among them a depressed economy and inflation. The already high food prices in Upper Silesia were driven even further upward by the Crimean War, which began in 1853. Because bread was needed for its soldiers, Russia, traditionally a source of cheap grain, prohibited grain exports. This forced grain prices skyward in Upper Silesia.

From the 1840's through 1850's Upper Silesia was racked by epidemics of cholera and typhus. To these health problems was added a great flood of the

9

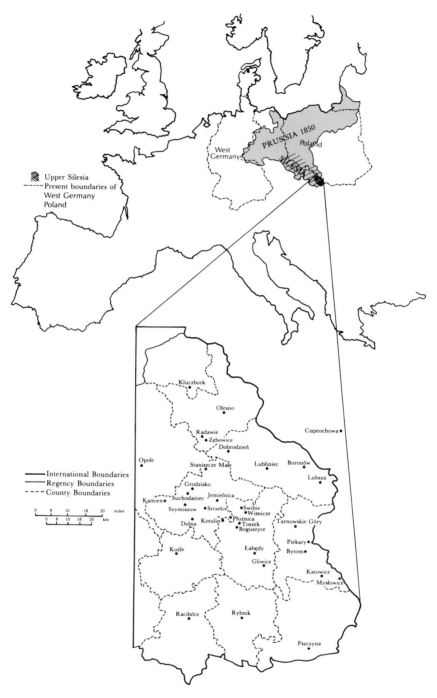

Upper Silesia
Present boundaries of
West Germany
Poland

PRUSSIA 1850

West
Germany

Poland

International Boundaries
Regency Boundaries
County Boundaries

0   8   10   18   20   miles
0   8   10   18   20   km

Kluczbork

Olesno

Radawie
Zębowice
Dobrodzień

Częstochowa

Opole

Staniszcze Małe   Lubliniec   Boronów

Lubsza

Grodzisko

Kamień

Suchodaniec   Jemielnica

Szymiszów   Strzelce   Świbie
Wiśnicze

Dolna   Kotulin   Płużnica   Tarnowskie Góry
Toszek
Boguszyce

Piekary

Koźle   Łabędy   Bytom

Gliwice

Katowice

Mysłowice

Racibórz   Rybnik

Pszczyna

10

A farm wagon in the yard of the inn at Płużnica, Poland

River Odra, the principal river of Silesia, in the summer of 1854. The inundation destroyed many of the crops and further increased the poverty of the region.

The emigrants who came to Texas did not fit the American stereotype of Slavic immigrants — poverty-ridden masses grasping for crusts of bread. They came from the peasant class, a group misunderstood by Americans both in the past and at the present. "Peasants" might best be described as members of the farming class. They were landowners, taxpayers, and far higher in social status than the landless laborers they employed. But the peasants were far lower in status than the nobles, to whom they bowed in almost hereditary deference. The Texas emigrants, although frightened by the economic problems in their homeland, were not yet seriously hurt by them. They departed Europe for Texas because they saw the route to economic advancement blocked in Europe but open to them in America. Instead of just wanting property, they wanted *more* property.

While the economic causes were the most important reasons for emigration from Upper Silesia to Texas, other factors also prompted the Polish farmers to leave. Among these was discrimination in which a minority German population was dominant over a Polish majority. The situation was described by a pastor among the Silesians in Texas during the middle years of the 1800's. He could calm even the most vocal complaints of the immigrants by reminding them of the social discrimination that they had suffered at the hands of the Germans in Upper Silesia:

> I thank you for your Prussian joys . . . and what freedom did you have? Didn't you have to work a great part only for the king? As soon as a boy grew up, they took him to the army, and for the defense of whom and what? Not your kingdom but the Prussion one. You lost your health and lives for what purpose? And taxes? Were they small? Did you forget how you were racked? You talked among yourselves that they took the holy pictures from the walls and covers from the beds of the poor. Wherever you went, you had to have a certificate from the officer of the Diet in the village.

Similarly, the editors of an Upper Silesian newspaper in the mid-19th century, commenting on the migration of Polish farmers to Texas, stated that the only reason they could imagine for the people to have gone to Texas was that in America they had "an equality of classes and greater freedom of life than here."

It is possible that the failure of the Revolution of 1848 to alleviate discrimination against the Poles in Upper Silesia may have contributed to the movement to Texas. At least one later immigrant to Texas, Stanisław Kiołbassa, had been

Bernard Kiołbassa and family

12

an active Polish nationalist during this period. He was elected to represent his district in Upper Silesia in the Prussian national parliament in 1848. Despite the fact that he could speak no language other than Polish, he participated in the activities of the parliament and served on the Committee for Mines and Foundries. When another deputy introduced a motion to have Kiołbassa expelled from the assembly because he could not communicate in German, other members came to his aid and defeated the attempt to have him unseated. Several years later in 1855 Kiołbassa and his family departed Silesia for Texas, where his descendants continue to live today.

Poles also left Silesia to evade conscription into the Prussian army, which was known throughout the world for its rigid discipline. At the age of 20 every young man in Prussia was subject to military draft. Active service lasted for three years, followed by two years in the active reserves and then 15 years in inactive reserves. Even men up to the age of 60 were liable to be called into service in the event of invasion. It was not uncommon for a father to send all but one of his sons abroad, leaving an "only son" who was exempt from duty. This was successful for several years, but when the authorities realized how men were evading the draft, the laws were changed so that the "only son" left in the country was no longer exempt.

Added to both the economic and social causes for emigration were a number of personal motives. Some people departed to escape scandals, to avoid family friction, to see new country,

Ignatius Burda in a Prussian army officer's uniform

because others had gone, and for dozens of other such reasons. Similarly, the decision to stay behind frequently was based on personal reasons. One man wrote from Texas back to Poland about his brother that "he doesn't want to come because he follows his wife's own ideas."

While these were the causes of emigration, other factors were significant both in starting and continuing the movement. These factors included favorable reports

13

from Texas, the efforts of emigration agents, and the spread of exaggerated rumors and stories painting the New World as a paradise.

Generally praising the new country, letters back to Europe were instrumental in encouraging others to leave for America. As early as February 1855 the high sheriff of an Upper Silesian county reported to higher authorities that the reason for movement from his district was reports from persons who had left the area and who wrote letters back home about their "well-being in America." By the next year the president of the Regency of Opole, the government district which

Interior of a restored 19th century Upper Silesian peasant cottage, located at the Museum of the Opole Countryside, Opole, Poland

encompassed the area sending emigrants, reported to Berlin that "favorable news" from Texas was increasing the tendency of the local farmers to leave the province.

Letters discussed agriculture, gave advice for travel, and described food in Texas. One peasant wrote to his family and friends in these words: "I talked with Joseph about it and he told me with tears in his eyes that it would be best if you came. When he came he was alone, but it was not so hard as in Silesia, because here he can breed whatever animals he wants and it costs nothing. He

14

told me that with the help of God he could sell his wheat for $100 . . . Come the sooner the better." The same man described agriculture in Texas this way: "If you have money, you can keep even 1,000 head of cattle, as the Americans do. You can plant cotton, which is very expensive, and I, John Moczygemba, plan to grow it."

Emigration agents, businessmen who represented shipping companies at the ports, made the way easier for the farmers to leave. As early as 1852 they had appeared in Upper Silesia and within three years were operating in the very towns and villages which were sending emigrants to Texas. The work of these entrepreneurs generally was criticized by their contemporaries who claimed that they duped the farmers into leaving their homes and booked their travel on unsafe ships. Not everyone was so critical, however, for one Silesian who emigrated described his agents as looking after his emigrants "as a father does for his children," while another wrote that his agent cared for "every person, even for the smallest child." Whether honest or not, emigration agents did provide a useful service to the departing farmers by facilitating their travel to the ports and from the ports to the Texas coast. Their contribution was in making the travel immediately possible and a bit easier.

During the 1850's the situation in Upper Silesia was ripe for the spread of stories about better life other places. Thus, tales about Texas were believed by the peasants. The countryside, in fact, was filled with rumors about Texas and a better life. Stories concerned free land, a Polish church waiting in America, and tales of "golden mountains," which most likely originated in the California gold rush half a decade before. Many of the farmers had no concept of how far they would be going or what problems they might encounter along the way. Some even thought they needed to go only to the nearest railway station from which they would go "directly to America."

Given the causes for emigration from Upper Silesia to Texas, together with the numerous promoting factors, the stage was set for increased migration. One important element was lacking — a catalyst to initiate the movement. This catalyst was to be a young Catholic priest, the Reverend Leopold Moczygemba.

Moczygemba was born in the Upper Silesian village of Płużnica, on the road between the county seat towns of Toszek and Strzelce Opolskie, on October 24, 1824. He spent his childhood in Płużnica and nearby Ligota Toszecka, where his father was an innkeeper and miller. He studied in the market towns of Opole and Gliwice, and then, at the age of 19, he decided to become a Catholic priest. In 1843 he traveled to northern Italy and became a member of the Order of Franciscans Minor Conventual. Studying several years in Italy, he completed his novitiate as a Friar and was ordained a priest. Because of his health he went to Wurzburg in Bavaria to complete his study. After a year there he transferred in 1849 to the Oggersheim monastery outside Mannheim.

Reverend Leopold Moczygemba

Ewa Moczygemba, mother of
Reverend Leopold Moczygemba

For several years Father Leopold dreamed of becoming a missionary in some distant part of the world, but neither his family nor his superiors felt that he was sufficiently prepared. He waited for an appropriate chance to present itself. Finally the opportunity came in the form of Bishop Jean-Marie Odin, the Bishop of Galveston in Texas. This Frenchman had returned to Europe in search of priests and monetary assistance for his far-flung diocese in the wilds of North America. Coming to Europe in 1852, he recruited numerous missionaries, among them four Franciscan Fathers and one lay brother to minister to the German immigrants in Texas. One of these Friars was 28-year-old Reverend Leopold Moczygemba. The missionaries sailed for America in the late summer of 1852, arriving in Galveston about the first of September.

The Friars were given custody of the German parishes in what then was considered to be west Texas. They received the churches at New Braunfels, Fredericksburg, Castroville, and D'Hanis, as well as a number of mission parishes to be served from these four. Father Moczygemba was assigned to New Braunfels, where he was the first resident Catholic pastor. Among his activities there was the complete transcription of the baptismal and marriage records which his visiting predecessors had prepared. Today one can read the early church records at Sts. Peter and Paul Church in New Braunfels in Father Moczygemba's clear handwriting. From New Braunfels Moczygemba moved to serve the Alsatians at Castroville in 1854.

16

Clearing the wilderness

Although living conditions were not easy on the Texas frontier in the 1850's, Father Moczygemba was able to observe the economic and social advancement of his German parishioners. He quickly realized that his family and friends could probably find the same success if they, too, came to Texas. Father Leopold began writing letters back to his friends and relatives in Upper Silesia, encouraging them to come to Texas. The letters were successful.

As early as the summer of 1854 groups of peasants in Upper Silesia were selling their properties in order to emigrate to Texas. That year approximately 150 farming families left for Texas; in 1855 about 700 people emigrated; and in 1856, the last year of mass migration, about 500 came to Texas. The local government authorities realized the importance of Father Leopold's letters in stimulating the movement. The high sheriff in one of the Upper Silesian counties reported

"New Braunfels," lithograph by Carl G. von Iwonski

17

to the police administration in Opole in the summer of 1855, that emigration from his district was being prompted by letters from "Father Moczygemba, who works in Texas and comes from Płużnica and has many relatives and friends in the Toszek region, who tries to persuade them to immigrate to America with prospects of a better life."

After having disposed of their property the first group of peasants left Upper Silesia in late September 1854. As they traveled through Berlin the press noted their passage: "On the 26th of September, 150 Poles from Upper Silesia arrived by train in Berlin and on the next day in the afternoon left by the Cologne Railway for Bremen, from where they plan to go by ship to Texas (to America)." The newspaper report continued: "This is worth mentioning because, as is known, Slavic people are so attached to their native land that emigration among them is extraordinary." After they arrived at Bremen they boarded the 265-ton wooden bark *Weser*, which, in October, departed on the two-month journey to Galveston. A small group of Silesian Poles, for reasons not known, failed to board the *Weser*, but sailed later on the brig *Antoinette*.

A surprising amount of information is available about the travel of these and later Polish emigrants from Upper Silesia to Texas. All the departing farmers, for example, traveled by train to the ports. Railway construction in Prussia in the 1840's and 1850's had made this form of travel comparatively easy and fast. The railway companies, in fact, encouraged departing emigrants to go by rail by offering them special rates and generous baggage allowances.

Most of the emigrants headed for Bremen as their port of departure, but a few of them chose other ports such as Hamburg or Szczecin. From these ports on the North European Plain, they generally sailed either to Galveston or to Indianola, although a few individuals found their way to New York or New Orleans. Soon Indianola became the favored port of arrival because of its nearness to San Antonio, only about two weeks away by oxcart. Father Moczygemba recommended Indianola to prospective settlers.

The typical voyage for the Silesian emigrants lasted about two months. They traveled in the steerage quarters of the sailing ships, a part of the vessels which took its name from the adjacent steering apparatus. It was a dark, windowless area which on the eastbound trips from America was filled with cargo bound for European ports. For the westbound trips, the area was fitted with rough board floors and platform-like bunk beds for carrying the emigrants, who spent most of their time below deck. Generally, two passengers were assigned to each bunk, which they padded with mattresses filled with sea grass or straw.

According to one of the firms which is known to have provided transportation for Poles to Texas, the meals on the ships were served "in abundance." Among the foods prepared by the ship's cook for the steerage passengers were salted beef, salted pork, potatoes, rice, barley, butter, beans, peas, sauerkraut, and dried

18

Indianola, looking east on Main Street, 1873

plums. The voyagers were permitted to bring along a limited amount of personal food. All the steerage passengers were expected to take turns in helping the cook prepare the communal meals.

The cost of passage from North Germany to Galveston in the mid-1850's varied from 35 to 45 gold talers, with children under the age of 10 having a 5-taler discount and infants traveling at no cost. The price of passage varied with the number of emigrants on each ship—the more passengers, the cheaper the fare. Along with the transportation each emigrant received a stipulated amount of baggage space both in the hold of the ship and in the steerage

Steerage bunks on an immigrant ship

19

quarters. The lighting of fires and the smoking of tobacco were prohibited on the ships, as was the carrying of either matches or gunpowder. Firearms had to be deposited with the captain for the duration of the voyage.

The letters from the settlers in Texas back to Upper Silesia give us a further view of what the immigration must have been like. Much of the advice concerned financial affairs. One Pole wrote home that the best money to take was "gold, and talers are good, but heavy." He then advised, "Don't take many bank notes, and if you have them, take only new ones." Other immigrants already in Texas recommended, "Take as much gold as you can . . . because you can make a profit from it." Father Moczygemba wrote candidly to his family, "Hide your money well," adding, "take care on the ship; the less company that you have the better." Yet another Pole in Texas wrote home to recommend that his family leave their legal affairs in proper order so as not to have any troubles with the local court. He also advised them to find a reliable emigration agent to arrange their travel and to "pay attention not to be cheated once more." One immigrant in Texas obviously wondering who would be coming from Poland, asked his addressee to "write who will come."

The immigration to Texas from Upper Silesia consisted of about 1500 individuals. Starting in 1854, it continued on a sizable scale until the winter of 1856–57, after which time immigration dwindled to only handfuls of peasants annually. Conditions both in Texas and in Upper Silesia contributed to the decline. In Texas the severe drought of 1856–57 caused the immigrants to cease encouraging their countrymen to join them, while in Upper Silesia improved economic conditions made staying at home more attractive than before.

After the first group of Silesians had arrived at Galveston in early December 1854, they secured transportation to Indianola farther down the coast, and then they turned inland to San Antonio. Numbering 159 they arrived in the Alamo City on December 21. Father Moczygemba came from Castroville to greet the new arrivals and to lead a part of their group to a place he had chosen for their main settlement. The site was about 60 miles to the southeast at the confluence of the San Antonio River and Cibolo Creek in the newly organized Karnes County. The group reached the place about Christmas-time, and Father Moczygemba offered a Christmas Mass for the group under the largest live oak tree at the site. Soon the location came to be known as Panna Maria, or Virgin Mary in Polish, and the community today has the distinction of being the oldest Polish settlement in the United States.

Most of the Poles who remained behind at San Antonio went in the opposite direction — west to the community of Bandera. It had been established in 1854 by Charles DeMontel, John James, and John H. Herndon, but raids by hostile Indians had threatened to force the inhabitants back east. The American promoters were more than pleased to help populate the place with the new Slavic immi-

"San Antonio de Bexar," lithograph by Hermann Lungkwitz

Galveston in 1852

grants. DeMontel provided them with transportation in wagons from San Antonio (some sources say Castroville) with the stipulation that none of the settlers could return in the wagons. As an American who witnessed their arrival recalled at a later date, "When these Polish people were dumped off here they had to stay, as they had no way to leave." At first the Silesians went to work for established residents in town and soon became substantial members of the community. Although it became the second permanent Polish colony in America, Bandera never had a large Polish population, having a total of only about 20 families by 1858.

A few of the Silesians, particularly craftsmen, stayed in San Antonio, where, within a dozen years, they had formed their own Polish Catholic parish and lived in a recognizable Polish Quarter. This Polish district remained a separate entity well into the 20th century, but today descendants of the Poles live in all parts of the city and no longer have their own separate church.

In 1855 immigrants from Upper Silesia established another pioneer Polish settlement in the state. Founded in eastern Bexar County that year, the colony was called Martinez for several years. In the late 1860's the Poles changed the name of the locality to Saint Hedwig, as it is known today. Saint Hedwig is the patron of Silesia, who is greatly revered by people in the region and whose grave has been a pilgrimage site for three centuries.

Charles S. DeMontel

Church of the Annunciation at St. Hedwig, 1925

First Years on the Frontier

The conditions that the Silesian peasants found on the Texas frontier were vastly different from those they had known in Europe. From a comparatively densely populated area divided between cultivated fields and regulated forests, they moved to areas of prairie, scrubby woods, and hills that were almost uninhabited. From soft, green Silesia they had moved into a raw wilderness.

One of the first needs felt by the immigrants was for shelter. In building they used methods of construction passed down for centuries in Europe. Usually the first house was a dugout covered with a straw thatch roof. One early settler recalled that the immigrants "lived in burrows, covered with brush stalks." Other settlers erected picket houses or, where the materials were available, built small log cabins. One American, recalling a visit to Panna Maria in 1855, said the peasants there "huddled together on little patches of land living in their pole cabins & sod houses." About the same time a Silesian wrote home to report that "here one can get a house very easily," because, he elaborated, "everybody builds his house for himself." Only in San Antonio did the immigrants find shelter available, but in the city a poor Mexican *jacal* hut cost as much as $5.00 to $6.00 a month to rent.

After a few months more substantial houses began to appear in the Polish communities. At least as early as 1858 stone residences began appearing, as did larger and more comfortable log houses. The fact that the farmers built their own houses

23

A thatch-roofed cellar similar to the houses first built by Polish settlers at Panna Maria

The John Gawlik house erected at Panna Maria in 1858, classic example of Upper Silesian folk architecture in a Texas setting

24

on their own land made a deep impression, as did the fact that they did not live in villages as they had in Europe. One of the Silesians wrote home, that "there are no villages . . . We live quite a distance from the church. It is farther than you live from the manor." In the mid-19th century the pastor at Panna Maria wrote to Europe that the homes of his parishioners were "hidden in the woods" outside the village and that mostly they were "made of wood, similarly to Lithuanian houses." About the same time the priest at Saint Hedwig wrote that in his community "the houses of the Poles are situated in the brush, far from the church, and all I can see are clouds and trees."

The houses that the immigrants built in Texas were remarkably similar to those used in Upper Silesia even today. They have steeply pitched roofs originally designed to allow snow to slip off easily, although snow is uncommon in the San Antonio area. Other striking elements of Upper Silesian architecture in Texas include the arrangement of rooms, rear roofs that reach very near to the ground, the location of ventilation openings for upper rooms, and meat-smoking rooms within the homes. Even though they have disappeared in Texas, thatch roofs were another interesting element of Polish rural architecture that survived in Texas into this century.

Of course, all the elements of Silesian peasant housing did not remain unchanged in Texas. The most prominent alteration in the style of architecture was the addition of porches to the south-facing, windward sides of the houses. The porches became standard on Polish houses in central Texas, and they undoubtedly were the most popular areas of the homes during nine months of the year. People enjoyed the cool shade of the porch and used the area for many of their activities: visiting, quilting, sewing, and occasionally sleeping.

Soon after the Poles arrived they had to make legal arrangements for the land where they wanted to live. Before they came Father Moczygemba had made preliminary arrangements, first planning to settle the Poles at a proposed town of Cracow near New Braunfels. For unknown reasons he abandoned this idea and then planned with John Twohig, an Irish-born banker and capitalist in San Antonio, to settle the Poles on land Twohig owned at the proposed Panna Maria settlement. It is not known whether the priest and the Irishman discussed land prices at this time, but after the Silesians arrived they were charged prices far in excess of other local land prices for the property at Panna Maria.

While other land in Karnes County was selling for less than $1.50 an acre, comparable land purchased by Poles at Panna Maria in sales completed before the Civil War averaged $5.88 per acre, with some farmers paying as much as $10.80 per acre. The cost of land at the other Polish colonies was much more reasonable: $1.00 to $2.00 an acre at Saint Hedwig and $2.00 an acre at Bandera. For the farmers at Panna Maria who could not afford Twohig's high prices, Father

John Twohig

F.V. Snoga's stone store at Panna Maria was constructed by John Twohig as a storage barn.

The Panna Maria countryside, looking toward the San Antonio River valley

Moczygemba bought a block of 238 acres. He retained 25 acres for the church and parceled out the remainder to immigrants who needed land.

Even before the Silesian farmers had made formal arrangements for their land, they had begun preparing it for planting. Very quickly the Poles adopted corn, the staple food crop in Texas, for both animals and men. One of the early settlers at Bandera recollected that an American neighbor by the name of Curtis introduced his family to roasting ears and that they had never seen anything like this food in Silesia. Several sources state that a Mexican rancher, Andreas Coy, gave the Panna Maria settlers their first corn for bread and seed.

The Polish immigrants cultivated a wide range of crops in Texas. One of them wrote home that the land was good and fertile, especially well suited for raising melons, potatoes, cucumbers, and pumpkins. Father Moczygemba, traveling in Europe in 1858, noted that the area settled by the Poles was particularly good for raising cotton, sugar cane, and tobacco. Although one of the immigrants wrote to Poland that he planned to raise cotton, its cultivation did not reach any sizable levels among the Poles until the years following the Civil War.

Livestock played an important role in Polish Texan agriculture for many years. Oxen were especially valued during the first years of settlement. Not only did they transport the immigrants and their possessions in carts from the coast, but they also provided the brute strength needed to break the unplowed soil, to move heavy timbers, and to do other heavy work. They had the further advantage of living on grass alone, not needing the grain required by other animals.

Oxen plowing near the Upper Silesian village of Sucho Daniec. Early Polish arrivals in Texas also used oxen as draft animals.

Cattle raised for meat also were important in the early days. Many of the Poles lived in areas which before their arrival had been used exclusively for raising livestock. On some farms the Poles adopted practices similar to those employed by the Americans who had held the land before them. Despite this fact, however, John Moczygemba obviously was still thinking in terms of European practice when he suggested that his cousin bring a boy from Poland as an indentured servant to tend cattle for him. Animal husbandry was especially important in the early years at the Saint Hedwig settlement. The mild climate and the fact that no permission was necessary to graze cattle on the unfenced prairies impressed one peasant so favorably that he wrote home: "You don't need to leave anything in the fields for feeding stock because there is very much for them far and near." Also, purchasing a milk cow was an important event for the immigrant families. A Bandera pioneer recalled that "we bought our first milk cow at Castroville . . . father went down there afoot and drove her home."

With the passage of years horses became the status symbols in the Polish immigrant communities, and they became the preferred animals for both agriculture and transportation. Some of them almost became family pets. Other animals frequently found on the Polish farms included chickens, ducks, geese, goats, and pet dogs.

During the initial years in Texas the dress of the Poles set them apart from the people who lived around them. Probably the best description of the clothing of the immigrants in the 1850's comes from L.B. Russell, who lived in Karnes County at the time that the Poles arrived. He recollected them wearing

". . . the costumes of the old country, many of the women having what at that time were regarded as very short skirts, showing their limbs two or three inches above the ankles. Some had on wooden shoes, and almost without exception they had broad-brimmed, low-crowned black felt hats, nothing like the hats then worn in Texas. They also wore blue jackets of heavy woolen cloth, falling just below the waist, and gathered into folds at the back with a band of the same material."

Quite a stir evidently was caused among the male portion of the American population by the short skirts of the Polish girls and women. Soon after they first arrived in Texas Father Moczygemba wrote back to his family saying, "Don't take any country dresses for Hanka, because she will not need them here. Our country dresses are the reason that the native people make fun of us and they cause sin."

Although it is a bit difficult for us today to imagine the Polish farmers clomping about the prairies in wooden shoes, such footwear was quite common in 19th century Silesia and remained in use there until after the Second World War.

Because they were on the frontier of settlement the Polish immigrants felt quite isolated. The great, open spaces both impressed the Poles and made them feel

An Upper Silesian peasant girl in folk dress *Silesian peasant girls near Opole bearing a decorated tree, the symbol of the coming spring*

uneasy. Expressing the isolation that he felt, one of the settlers wrote home to Poland about the northern United States being "as far away as we are from you."

Thus, the immigrants, quite understandably, were afraid of attacks from the Indians. They were wise to be cautious, for Indians not only raided around them, but they also attacked the Poles. These raids were the most serious at Bandera, the most exposed of all the Silesian settlements, and the fear of attack became a part of the lives of the Poles living there for a full 20 years.

In a typical attack Albert Haiduk was wounded not far from his home at Bandera. Hearing what he presumed to be cattle breaking into his cornfield one night, he went out to drive them away, only to see three Indian warriors coming toward him from across the field. He hid behind a tree, and the first two of the three raiders passed by him. The third, however, saw him behind the tree and shot an arrow into his side. Fortunately Haiduk turned to one side as the Indian shot the arrow, and it did not penetrate too deeply. The injured man made it back to his cabin, where, without any light (for fear of attracting the Indians), his wife cut the arrow from his side using a small knife.

Other Silesians were not so fortunate. The best-known Silesian victim of the Indians was a 25-year-old Polish shepherd named Theodore Kindla, who was attacked near his sheep camp in the Sabinal Canyon southwest of the Bandera colony. He was surprised by a group of warriors as he scouted from his camp in search of a new water hole. A Mexican companion saw the Indians in time to hide, but Kindla did not see them until it was too late. The Mexican watched

29

"Preparing the Ambush," engraving by W.M. Cary

in horror at the event that followed. The attackers first roped the Pole to prevent him from escaping, then lanced him several times and shot a number of arrows into him. Then, as he lay on the ground, still alive, they scalped him and peeled the skin from the bottoms of his feet.

Leaving him for dead, the attackers moved on. Kindla, however, had survived their tortures, and he attempted to stagger back to his camp, succeeding only in going a few hundred feet. After the Indians had gone and the Mexican herder felt the area was safe, he went to Kindla's aid only to find him dead. Hastening to the town to warn others of the danger, the Mexican returned the next day leading a party of settlers. They found the young man's body already so decomposed that they had to bury him in the ground where he had fallen.

In a later incident the Indians attacked the Catholic pastor at Bandera in the rectory inside the town. Breaking out the windows and shooting at him with bows and arrows, the attackers were held back by the priest using his rifle. Finally a party of Silesians came to his rescue, driving the Indians away.

Although Indians posed a more dangerous threat, the Polish settlers were also terrified by the rattlesnakes they found in the area where they settled. Probably the fact that the immigrants had not known such reptiles in Europe caused them to fear them so much in Texas. The apprehension that the immigrants felt for

30

the vipers was well expressed by one of them a century ago: "There was tall grass everywhere, so that if anyone took a few steps he was soon lost to sight. Every step of the way you would meet rattlesnakes . . . . And several died of snakebites . . . . Everybody without exception had to carry a stick, hoe, or pitchfork wherever he took a step as protection against snakes." Stories have survived up to this day about encounters with rattlesnakes. One of these concerns Father Moczygemba, who had planned a dinner to welcome to Texas a group of newly arrived immigrants. They complained to him about the conditions they had found in Texas, but Father Leopold succeeded in calming them. Then, just as he was serving the soup, a big rattlesnake tumbled down from the rafters onto the table. As a Pole recounted the story: "How they shrieked until they could get out of the hut!"

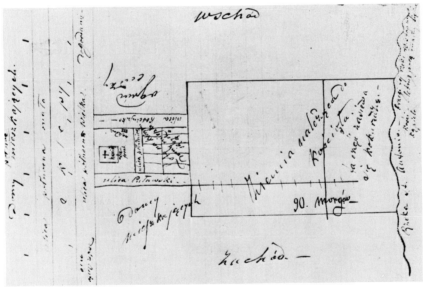

Father Adolf Bakanowski's plan of Panna Maria, prepared in April 1869

One of the immediate goals of the Silesians was the establishment of churches and schools. The first church to be erected was at Panna Maria. In March 1855 Father Moczygemba purchased land, and in May of that year he was already busy examining stone to be used for construction. As a result of various problems, not the least of them securing building materials and illness of workers, the construction was conducted in stages. The first began in summer 1855, when Father Moczygemba entered into a contract with a German stonemason from San Antonio, but it ended with the walls only about 15 feet high and all the builders too ill to work. Work stopped for several months. Then in early 1856

the effort was renewed with another mason, this time a Polish immigrant named John Gawlik, who had just arrived from Upper Silesia. The new mason completed the walls up to their planned 20-foot height, but again work lapsed, this time because lumber ordered for the roof had not arrived. Then Gawlik fell ill. When the wood finally did arrive Father Leopold was forced to make another agreement in hopes of completing the project. The third agreement was with another German from San Antonio, a Mr. Stark, who cut the wood, but did not finish the job. In the end Moczygemba made an agreement with an Upper Silesian immigrant, Gerwazy Gabrys, who finished the roof sometime in mid-summer 1856. With the shell of the building complete, a Mr. Boden from San Antonio made the frames for the windows and doors, completed the doors and floor in the sacristy and room of the priest, and built stairs to the priest's room located above the sacristy. By September 1856 the structure was finished, even though only linen

Church of the Immaculate Conception of the Blessed Virgin Mary at Panna Maria

covered the windows and the sanctuary had no benches, floor, or choir. Father Moczygemba blessed the building on September 29, dedicating it to "the glory of Almighty God and the Blessed Virgin Mary," and the oldest Polish parish in America received its first church. The structure continued to serve the parish until the 1870's, when it was severely damaged by lightning and then completely rebuilt. This reconstructed building, several times enlarged, continues to serve the Panna Maria parish today.

Soon the settlers at Bandera and Saint Hedwig began the construction of their own churches. The Bandera Poles began their project in 1858 under the guidance of Father Anthony Rossadowski, who took Father Moczygemba's place as priest for the Polish Texans. The building at Bandera was a small log cabin, but it served the religious needs of the community until the 1870's when Father Felix Zwiardowski supervised the construction of the present stone church for St. Stanislaus parish, the second oldest Polish parish in America. The Saint

Parishioners at the St. Stanislaus Catholic Church in Bandera, 1915

*Reverend Felix Zwiardowski as
a young man*

St. Michael's Catholic Church at San Antonio

Hedwig Poles began their church in either 1856 or 1857 on land which had been donated by one of the settlers. They amazed their Texas neighbors by the way they were able to move the large timbers for the building with their oxen as they erected the log church, which was used until after the Civil War, at which time it also was replaced. The San Antonio Poles did not have their own separate church until 1866, when they began having their own religious services in a former bakery and warehouse in the Polish Quarter of the city. Before this time they had attended Masses read by visiting Polish priests in San Fernando Church on the main plaza of San Antonio.

Although information concerning it is limited, it is clear that a Polish school

San Fernando Cathedral at San Antonio

35

Students of St. Joseph's School at Panna Maria

existed at Panna Maria at least as early as 1858. In that year Father Moczygemba visited Europe and was interviewed by newspaper correspondents to whom he related that there was a "small school" at the colony and that he planned to "take a young Pole to be a teacher" there. Another source from the 19th century reports that Peter Kiołbassa served as teacher in the community "under Father Anthony Rossadowski," who was priest among the Polish Texans from 1856 to 1860. Kiołbassa was the son of the deputy to the Prussian parliament in 1848, who had come to Texas in 1855.

After the Civil War when Polish missionaries from the Congregation of the Resurrection came to Texas, a permanent two-story stone school building was built at Panna Maria, and it served the community for many years. Today a new school building stands near the old one which is now a historical museum.

Probably the most important factor in closing immigration from Upper Silesia to Texas was the great drought of 1856–57, one of the most severe droughts in Texas history. The bad weather started before Christmas 1855, when a series of wet, cold northers swept across the state. The fronts followed one another until late March 1856, setting back planting several weeks. Then at the time the late crops were maturing, the drought set in. By late summer the local press complained that the weather was the driest in the memory of the oldest settlers and that even the best wells in the area were going dry. This was only the start, for the dry weather continued for a year. Several sources agree that 14 months passed with no rain whatsoever at the Panna Maria colony, while in the prairies around Seguin, only about 20 miles from Saint Hedwig, the ground cracked open as much as a foot wide and 30 to 40 feet deep.

With the drought came inflation and high food prices. Corn in San Antonio reached the price of $2.00 a bushel, while only a few months before it sold at 75 cents for the same amount. In rural Karnes County the same grain during the peak of the drought sold for $3.00 a bushel, and flour cost an incredible $24.00 per barrel. Because of the inflated food prices some of the immigrants may indeed have suffered from hunger. A local American noted that "had it not been for the abundance of wild game" the new immigrants "would have starved to death." In order to earn even a marginal income, many of the Silesians went to work for other area residents, men working on farms and ranches and women working as domestic servants.

An unexpected result of the drought was a break in relations between Father Moczygemba and the people he had brought to Texas. The settlers had perhaps expected an idyllic land and found a rough frontier. From the early days of settlement the immigrants had complained about conditions to Moczygemba, but their discontent broke into personal hostility against the priest in 1856. The priest, who had become the superior of the Franciscan missions in Texas, was caught between responsibilities to "his" people and to his religious order. For months he wrote to Rome requesting "a Polish father" to care for the Silesians in order for him to fulfill his duties as superior. But he received responses to his letters only rarely, and then, there was very little assistance. Finally another priest, Father Anthony Rossadowski, did arrive, and Moczygemba departed Panna Maria for

Reverend Leopold Moczygemba in later life

Marianna Moczygemba Wrobel and her daughter Ewa Wrobel, sister and niece of Rev. Leopold Moczygemba, Poland, 1880's

the German settlements in the state. A number of sources state that his very life may have been in danger, as some of the colonists wanted to hang the priest, and others wanted to drown him in what little water remained in the San Antonio River. Father Leopold left Panna Maria in October 1856 and departed Texas entirely in 1858, to return later only for brief visits. The anger of the immigrants remained strong for a number of years, for in 1867 missionaries reported to Rome that the Silesians "cannot forgive him up to this day" for having brought them to Texas.

The anger had abated by the 1870's, however, for Moczygemba was able to return to the settlements in 1874 to visit with his brothers and their families, and in 1877 to witness the blessing of the cornerstone of the new church at Panna Maria. He spent most of his later life working among German, Italian, and Polish immigrants in the northern United States. He was co-founder of the Polish seminary at Detroit, and he helped organize the Polish Roman Catholic Union, the largest Polish Catholic organization in the United States. Moczygemba died near Detroit in 1891 and was buried in that city.

Expansion of Silesian Settlement

During the 19th century Silesian Polish settlement expanded both in the San Antonio area and elsewhere in the state. Among the new Polish communities were those at Meyersville and Yorktown in DeWitt County. As early as 1856 Poles had begun moving to these two areas which already had been settled by Germans. In time, antagonism developed between the two groups over the question of language use in the Meyersville church. In the end the Meyersville Silesians moved their religious affiliation to the Catholic parish in Yorktown, which after the Civil War had its own church and school. As a result Yorktown, which the Silesians called Jordan, became the center of Polish ethnic affairs in the DeWitt County area, a role that it continues to play to this day. In the 1860's a number of Polish families moved near the Coleto community in DeWitt County, and for many years visiting Polish priests served the inhabitants of the area, but with the passage of time its population merged with the people around it, and Coleto lost its Polish identity.

A series of Polish communities at one time existed along the Gulf Coastal Plain of Texas. The easternmost of these communities was Saint Francisville, located near present Bay City in Matagorda County. Traditional accounts state that the community was founded by stragglers who felt that they could not make the complete journey from Galveston to San Antonio. Known by the Americans as the "Polish Village," the community had its own church but never had the financial resources to keep its own pastor. Among the names of Polish families in the community were Gola, Sisky, Ryman, Bonk, Waschka, and Petrucha. At the

Farm scene near Yorktown

present time the old wooden church beside the cemetery at Saint Francisville stands empty except on All Souls Day, when the Silesians gather annually to tend the graves of their ancestors and to attend a Mass in remembrance of them.

Also on the Gulf Coastal Plain were Silesian Polish communities at Inez and Victoria. Inez, known at the time by the Poles as Gazeta from the local name, Garcitas, had about a dozen Polish families who were visited by traveling Polish priests as late as the 1870's. Victoria, which had a much larger general population, had a number of Polish families. In the 1860's the community had over a dozen Silesian families and ties so strong to the other colonies that at least one of its daughters left to join a Polish convent which had been established in Panna Maria. Polish priests also visited Victoria regularly well into the 1870's.

In Atascosa County, to the south of San Antonio, the Poles established a colony at Las Gallinas. Known by the immigrants as Gaina, the community was located in range country. It numbered as many as 25 families and also through the 1870's was visited by traveling Polish priests, although like many of the other small Polish colonies, it today has lost its Slavic ethnic identity.

As a result of the suffering from the drought of 1856–57, some Silesian immigrants departed Texas entirely. Traveling north to a place near the Missouri River

40

west of St. Louis, they founded a colony in Franklin County, Missouri, which they called Krakow. They were joined by immigrants from other parts of Poland and expanded their settlement area to include the communities of Owensville and Clover Bottom. Contact remained between the Silesians of Texas and of Missouri, with visits of individuals between the colonies through the years. A former schoolmaster from Panna Maria edited a newspaper in Franklin County, and there was even a "pilgrimage to Panna Maria" organized by local people in 1973.

Silesian Polish settlement areas continued to expand in Texas during the later years of the 1800's as well as in the current century. The next major Silesian settlement founded in Texas was at Czestochowa, about five miles upstream from Panna Maria on Cibolo Creek. By 1873 there were enough Polish farmers in the area to establish a school, which served the additional purpose of being a chapel to which the pastor from Panna Maria made a monthly visit for Sunday Mass. On other Sundays the farmers from the upper valley had to go on foot or in wagons to the mother colony. When the church at Panna Maria was seriously damaged by lightning and had to be rebuilt, the farmers at Czestochowa decided that they would be wiser to spend their money building a new church within their community, thus causing a measure of bad feeling with the people at Panna Maria. Despite the

The Black Madonna, or
Our Lady of Częstochowa

opposition, however, the Czestochowa farmers did build their own church, which was dedicated in 1878. Several months later, as a sign of their reconciliation, the parishioners from Panna Maria presented to the new parish a large painting of the Virgin of Częstochowa, the patroness of Poland.

The next settlement founded in the valley of Cibolo Creek was Kosciuszko, located in Wilson County a few miles farther up the valley. It was founded in 1892, when a Polish school was built there. The community was named for Tadeusz Kosciuszko, hero of both the American Revolution and the Polish Insurrection against the Russians that began in 1792, the centenary of which was being

The old convent building at Czestochowa

Church of the Nativity of the Blessed Virgin Mary at Czestochowa, consecrated in 1878, later expanded

celebrated by Poles around the world at that time. The school was followed by the building of a church in 1898.

The last Polish colony founded in the Cibolo Valley was in Stockdale, a community already established by Americans years before Silesians began moving into the area in the late 19th century. The Poles there erected a small chapel, which was served by priests from Kosciuszko, but they never had the ability to support their own pastor.

Convenient transportation for agricultural products brought a number of younger Poles from the older settle-

Thaddeus Kosciusko, Polish hero of the American Revolution

ments to a new town named Falls City, founded in 1884 on a siding of the San Antonio and Aransas Pass Railroad between San Antonio and the Gulf of Mexico. The movement to the new town, a few miles west of the Cibolo Creek settle-

The City Saloon at Falls City, 1921

43

ments, doomed Czestochowa and Panna Maria to economic stagnation, while Falls City became the center of business for the Karnes and Wilson County Poles. From 1902 the Falls City Poles had their own Polish church and Polish schools.

Outside the area of general Polish settlement is the White Deer colony. Located in the northern Texas Panhandle, the Polish community was founded in 1909. In that year three young men from Panna Maria set out for west Texas to explore the possibilities for beginning a Polish settlement in the region. They were joined at Rhineland in Knox County by another young Silesian, whose family had moved there, and the four headed northwest toward the Panhandle. Two of the men found work in the wheat harvest, one returned home to help with the cotton harvest, but one, Henry Czerner, remained to search for land. After discussions with a number of land agents and promoters, he met Timothy Dwight Hobart, who represented the White Deer Land Company. Hobart agreed to give the Poles an option on a large block of land in the vicinity of the White Deer community, and that very year Poles began leaving south Texas for the Panhandle.

Henry Czerner and Ben Urbanczyk

Wedding of Mary Gordzelik and Henry Czerner at White Deer, 1912

By 1916 about 20 Polish families had settled at White Deer, but because the others were slow in coming the land company put the remaining acreage up for public sale, and others purchased all of it within six months. One of the first things done by the Poles of White Deer as an organized group was the construction of a church. In 1911 they purchased land for it on the north side of the town, and by 1913 they had built the structure. The Poles at White Deer continue to be an active group, and their annual harvest festival each autumn is well known throughout the region.

44

The experiences of the Vincent Haiduk family give us some idea of what it must have been like to settle at White Deer in the early years of this century. In November 1910 the family moved from Panna Maria area to White Deer in two railway boxcars. Most of the family, including seven children, their furniture, personal belongings, and 450 bushels of shelled corn, rode in one of the cars. The other boxcar carried one son, Ben, and all the livestock, which had to be watered at each stop along the way.

After they arrived at White Deer the Haiduk family spent the next months with one of their daughters, Rosie, who had married John Urbanczyk. The only building at the farmstead was a granary, which to the great discomfort of the residents faced the north and the cold, icy blasts of wind. During the day the parents sent the children to walk along the railroad tracks to pick up pieces of coal which dropped from the passing railway cars to fuel the one big stove that sat in the center of the granary. Rosie Haiduk Urbanczyk was not at all happy with her husband for having brought her to the windswept, treeless plains, and she complained to him: "We have four children and there ain't nothing here." Her husband replied that, despite the uncompromising surroundings, they were going to stay and "going to make it." In later life Rosie reminisced, "So we made it," adding with pride, "We had the first Catholic child born in White Deer."

John Urbanczyk and family

The Civil War Years

During the 1850's the Poles and the Texans usually just eyed each other with curiosity and from some distance. One man who accidentally rode into the Panna Maria settlement in 1855 recollected in later years: "In the month of November . . . we came upon some dugouts not far from the Cibolo, but we found people there that couldn't understand what we said to them . . . . They might have come from the moon or stars for what we knew or could find out." Of such encounters one of the Silesians recalled: "Sometimes one of the Americans would appear. We couldn't talk with them, so they just gazed at us in wonder, smiled, and . . . went away."

The feelings of many of the "native" Texans in the 1850's were prejudiced, however. During these years in San Antonio there were a number of incidents in which, for example, young troublemakers pelted both students and teachers at a Catholic boys' school with stones. Intoxicated riders attempted to go on horseback into the Catholic churches during religious services. At least some of the negative actions were directed specifically against the Poles. About the same time that the third group of Silesians were arriving in Texas the local newspaper in San Antonio carried reports of public speakers warning "the late immigrants from Poland . . . not to settle in this section."

The Silesians in Texas, for the most part, probably did not even know it when the Civil War began in 1861. It was early in this year that the citizens of the state voted overwhelmingly in favor of secession from the Union. The Silesian

47

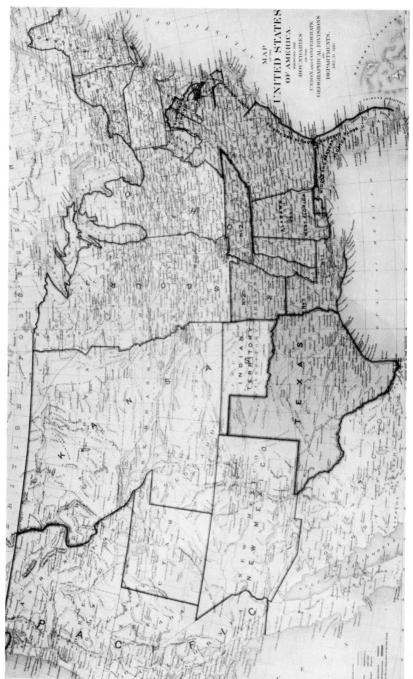

Boundaries of the Union and Confederate geographical divisions

48

immigrants had not been in the state long enough to have become voters, and, furthermore, most of them still spoke only Polish. The war years were difficult for the immigrants. Many of them despaired as the conflict dragged on and on, seemingly forever. One of the Poles later related that "we were looking forward to our end."

Most of the Silesians were either indifferent toward the Confederate government or openly opposed to it. These feelings probably were not based on their opposition to the institution of slavery, although no Silesian slaveholders have been identified, but rather from the fact that many of them had come to America so they or their sons could avoid conscription into the Prussian army in Europe. They did not want to fight in anyone else's wars, either in the Old World or in the New. Tales still told in Polish Texan families attest to the fact that the Silesians tended to avoid all Confederate officials — especially conscription officers.

Relations became particularly strained between the two groups during the Civil War years. This situation became even more serious when it was learned that some of the Silesians had deserted from the Confederate Army to fight on the side of the North. This information became common knowledge in the spring of 1863, when the local San Antonio newspaper published the names of certain soldiers who had changed sides. The list included several Silesians.

Also presenting problems on the home front were the shortages and inflation of the wartime economy, the effects of which already were becoming evident in south Texas by the second year of the conflict. By this time flour was selling for $40 a barrel in San Antonio, cornmeal sold for $2.50 per bushel, and coffee went for between $7.00 and $9.00 a pound, or for $1.00 in gold outside the city. Footwear became especially expensive, with shoes costing $8.00 to $10.00 a pair and a pair of boots selling for $20. If these difficulties were not already enough, the area south of San Antonio to the Mexican border, especially after the fall of Brownsville to Union forces in 1863, became infested with renegades and ban-

A United States-Mexican boundary survey team at Brownsville

49

dits that preyed on the settlements in the area—many of them places inhabited predominantly by Poles.

Coupled with the economic problems and difficulties with the Americans and renegades, the war years saw a recurring drought. This time the dry period began in 1862 and continued through 1865. Even though occasional rains relieved the suffering for brief periods of time, most of the streams remained dry, and livestock wandered off in all directions looking for both grass and water. As one American who lived in Karnes County at the time recalled, the San Antonio River dried up entirely and "stunk with carrion from its head to its mouth."

If all this were not already enough to cause the Silesians to despair, in 1863 they lost their only Polish priest. Father Julian Przysiecki had come to Texas as early as 1857 and from 1860 onward, through the war years, he was the only Polish clergyman in the state. He rode on horseback to serve the Poles from Panna Maria over 100 miles to Bandera. The pastor was killed in a riding accident at the Saint Hedwig community in 1863, where his grave may be seen today. His death left the Silesians without a resident Polish pastor for three years.

To keep their faith alive, the Poles met in the little churches to recite the rosary, sing hymns, and chant the Mass in the vernacular, while at least some of their urgent religious needs were met by visiting priests, most of them French or German Benedictines from San Antonio.

Although the Silesians attempted to avoid conscription into the Southern army, a considerable number of them did fight for the Confederacy. One such person

Peter Kiołbassa dressed as a Union soldier   *John Moczygemba in Confederate uniform*

50

was Albert Lyssy, an 18-year-old Pole from Karnes County. He was registered for the draft in Karnes County in February 1862 and then was conscripted into the 24th Texas Cavalry two months later. The unit was ordered to the Arkansas Post, a reinforced earthen fortress up the Arkansas River from its mouth on the Mississippi. Reaching there by October 1862, the unit spent time drilling and building up the defenses of the fort against an expected Union attack. Life must not have been too unpleasant for the men, for the winter was mild, and when cool nights did come the troops had comfortable quarters in log cabins which had been covered with split boards. They seemed satisfied with their rations of pumpkins, cornbread, and sorghum.

The Union attack on Fort Hindman near Arkansas Post, 1863

The expected federal attack came on January 10, 1863, at which time gun-boats started bombarding the Arkansas Post with cannon fire, and federal troops began landing below it. The next morning the Union forces began attacking the fortress from both land and water. The Union forces greatly outnumbered the Southerners, and most of the men in gray knew that they would not be able to hold out indefinitely against their blue-clad enemy. As the federal troops were preparing for another charge on the Confederate positions, without warning white flags appeared among the men of the 24th Texas Cavalry. Before the Southern officers could suppress the flags of surrender, Union soldiers crowded the lines and made the capitulation complete. Thus unidentified members of Lyssy's own unit effected the surrender of the Arkansas Post and the capture of most of its 5,000 defenders.

Without delay the Confederate troops were ordered to stack their arms. That night they slept on the bank of the river, and the next morning they were placed on troop transports and sent down the Arkansas and then up the Mississippi to prisoner-of-war camps in the northern states. Lyssy and a substantial number of his fellow prisoners, however, were not destined to sit out the remainder of the war in a prisoner-of-war camp.

Union army officers already were discussing what to do with the foreign-born men who had been captured at the Battle of Arkansas Post. On the fourth of February 1863 the commander of Camp Butler, Illinois, wrote to one of his superiors that many of the men held at the camp had been "pressed" into the rebel army and that they were "anxious to take the oath of allegiance" to the Union and join loyal federal regiments in camp nearby. He noted specifically that these men were "foreigners, Germans, Polanders, etc." At the same time the camp quartermaster made a similar report. Within a short time, as a result of these requests, the commander of the United States Army Department of the Ohio issued orders that all the men in the camps who had been "forced against their will to serve in the rebel army" should be released and allowed to enter Union regiments. Thus, within only a few days of their capture, Albert Lyssy and a number of his compatriots were allowed out of the prisoner-of-war camps.

The last national flag of the Confederacy

After his release Lyssy joined the 16th Illinois Cavalry, where he served as a private in Company G for a year. Then on May 12, 1864, he was captured again, this time by the Confederates. The capture took place near Tunnel Hill, not far from Dalton, Georgia, and at the time Lyssy was injured by two gunshot wounds, one in the hip and another shattering the bones just above his right wrist. A prisoner of war for the second time, Lyssy stayed a captive of the Confederates until almost the end of the war, when he was returned to Union hands in an exchange of prisoners. While he was a prisoner of war in the South, Albert received only limited attention to his injured arm and wrist, causing them to grow together abnormally. After this happened nothing could be done to repair the damage. Returning to Union forces on February 26, 1865, Lyssy went first to Benton Barracks, Missouri, and then to Nashville, Tennessee, where he was mustered out of service on August 19, 1865. He made his way back to Karnes County, but he was never able to return to his former occupation as a carpenter because of the injury to his arm. He was forced to leave the skilled job for that of a teamster, where his right arm was needed less.

Another young Silesian who fought in the Confederate Army was Alexander Dziuk. As a boy he had immigrated to Texas from the Upper Silesian village of Płużnica in the 1850's and had settled with his family in Karnes County. As an older man he remembered the war years: "At the age of eighteen . . . I was drafted into the Confederate Army and sent to Arkansas . . . . We were badly fed, especially at the beginning, and were armed with old flintlocks . . . . I remained in the Confederate Army until the end of the war and when I got back home even my own mother could not recognize me." The probable reason that his mother had difficulty in recognizing her son was that he had suffered serious lung ailments in the army and lost a considerable amount of weight. His lung problems were so severe, in fact, that he was given a disability discharge from one of the units in which he served. Despite the health problems, however, Dziuk lived to a ripe old age and became one of the most influential settlers in the Panna Maria colony during the later years of the 19th century.

Not all the Silesians who fought in the war for the side of the North did so by changing from one side to the other. Some of them entered the federal service directly, as did Joseph Cotulla, for whom the south Texas town of Cotulla was eventually named. Joseph had come to Texas from Upper Silesia in 1856. The year before, some of his family members had preceded him. Later he, his mother, and his grandmother sailed to Texas on the bark *Von Bealieu,* and then they trekked to the Las Gallinas settlement in Atascosa County, where the other members of the family had settled. In the second year of the Civil War young Joseph Cotulla left his Las Gallinas home in the company of six companions, all of whom headed for the Rio Grande and Mexico. They crossed the border and headed for Matamoros, where the group split up. Cotulla crossed the river into Brownsville, which by that time was already in federal hands, and he volunteered to serve in the

1st Texas Cavalry in the Union Army, a unit composed primarily of Texans who supported the North. He sailed under orders to New Orleans, met members of his regiment, and then spent the next two years in the United States Army, seeing action mostly in Louisiana. Cotulla received his discharge in San Antonio at the end of the war and returned to his home in south Texas, where he became a prominent rancher.

Joe Cotulla and family at their ranch home near Cotulla

The Poles were greatly relieved by the close of the war in late spring of 1865. They saw the federal victory as an act of God in his mercy relieving their long suffering. As one Pole recollected: "At last God took pity on us: The Confederacy was defeated." Even though the end of hostilities did not solve all the problems that the Silesians faced, it did bring most of the Polish soldiers back from the battlefields to their families, and this probably was the most important thing for both the men and their families.

Reconstruction for the Silesian Poles in Texas

The Reconstruction period, the name generally given to the years immediately following the Civil War, was probably the time of the greatest social unrest in the entire history of the state of Texas. As the war ended, the Confederate administration which had existed in the state deteriorated. Lawlessness became rampant, and finally there were no legally constituted bodies to restrain it. The situation became so bad, for example, that robbers were able to break into the state capitol in Austin to steal the last gold money that the state possessed. It was not until June 19, 1865, that the first federal troops arrived in Texas to declare officially the authority of the United States over the former rebellious state. It was still several weeks before United States troops began reaching many of the inland points to start restoring order.

Complicating the army's efforts to bring the lawlessness under control was the fact that most white Texans resented the soldiers' presence. The Texans offered very little resistance, but only because they lacked the force to do otherwise. To the typical Southerner, the acts of the United States Congress were viewed as hostile, and the loss of their voting rights and the granting of these rights to the freed slaves were seen as acts of insult and oppression.

The lawless conditions in the state affected virtually all the Silesians either directly or indirectly. In almost all the settlements Poles fell victims to thieves, robbers, and even murderers. In urban San Antonio, in an incident common at the time, Jacob Kyrish was severely hurt when he was mugged on a city street, while for several weeks during 1869 a group of thieves operated in the area of the Polish Quarter of the city, as the local press noted, working "near the Polander church, stealing everything they can get hold of."

At Saint Hedwig an elderly Pole was the victim of Bill Thompson, brother of the notorious Texas badman, Ben Thompson. Falsely claiming to be a deputy sheriff, the outlaw "arrested" a man and charged him with stealing fence rails, and then he "arrested" several former slaves and stole their guns. Next the hoodlum came upon the old Silesian, a man in his eighties, and tried to rob him. The Silesian was defiant, so Thompson shot him in the arm and side and then moved on to harass others. For several days he and his gang of toughs terrorized the road between San Antonio and Helena, the county seat of Karnes County.

Reverend Adolf Bakanowski

As if such incidents were not serious enough, in Karnes County the difficulties took on a serious political cast. The area was known through the state at the time as a lawless place, and by chance it happened to be a center of Unionist Silesian sentiment. Clearly trouble was bound to erupt between the resentful, defeated Southerners and the "scalawag foreigners" who supported the Union. As a sympathetic Northern observer noted at the time, "They seem to have settled the meanest place in Texas." Father Adolf Bakanowski, the pastor at Panna Maria from 1866 to 1870, the peak of the troubles, later remembered the situation:

They knew that we Poles held with the side of the North, so that was why they considered us their enemies. . . . They began to make every effort to drive them (the Poles) from the country, even by force of arms . . . . When they saw a Pole without knowledge of the language, a peasant with no education, these Southerners looked upon him as they did upon the Blacks, and felt that they had the same right to deny him his human rights as they did the Blacks.

Helena, the county seat, only four miles from Panna Maria, was the center of the rebellious feelings. It furthermore had a statewide reputation as a rough town. Even though the ordinary occupation of the inhabitants generally was stock

The old Karnes County courthouse at Helena

raising, a German immigrant, who settled there in 1868, noted that they most enjoyed stealing horses and raiding the freight wagons that passed along the near-by road inland from the coast. A Northern sympathizer who passed through the area about the same time described Helena as "a mean little Confed town, with 4 stores, 4 whisky mills, and any amount of lazy vagabonds laying around, living by their wits."

Violence first erupted between the Southerners and the Poles over the question of voting rights. As new officials registered loyal citizens to vote in the summer of 1867, they permitted only freed Negroes and supporters of the Union to sign up. Among these "loyal" voters were newly naturalized Silesians who had never voted before. During the registration at Panna Maria, a group of Southerners rode in on horseback from Helena, acted abusively toward the registrars, and actually beat two newly naturalized immigrants who, as the cowboys jeered, wanted to make "d--d Yankees" out of themselves. One of the Southern party announced before all present that he would wager any amount of money that after only two months no one who took any oaths of allegiance to the United States would be left in the town.

This incident was only the first of many in which the cowboys from Helena harassed the Silesians. On numerous occasions the cowboys would ride into the Polish village roping the children and shooting their pistols at the feet of any peasants they happened to meet. In one incident they rode on horseback into the church at Panna Maria during the Mass and conducted themselves in an obscene way. When Polish men were not at home the other locals were known

57

to ride up to the houses and bang on the shutters to frighten the women and children inside, while they also enjoyed the sport of riding up to open fires where women were cooking or washing in order to throw a handful of bullets into the fires just to see the foreigners run for shelter. In an especially cruel incident, a party of toughs rode up to a Polish girl who was milking the family cow. They frightened her severely, threatening to shoot her on the spot, and then, without warning, killed the milk cow at her side.

The harassment continued until the spring of 1869 when, after a large group of armed Southerners had harassed the entire Panna Maria community on Easter Sunday, the Poles requested military protection from the United States Army authorities in San Antonio. Apparently unknown to the Poles, plans already had been made for the establishment of an army camp near rebellious Helena. Thus, on April 10, 1869, the army came to Karnes County, and the temporary Post of Helena was established at least in part for the protection of the loyal Silesian farmers. Within a year the troops had restored Karnes County to order, and the camp was abandoned as no longer necessary.

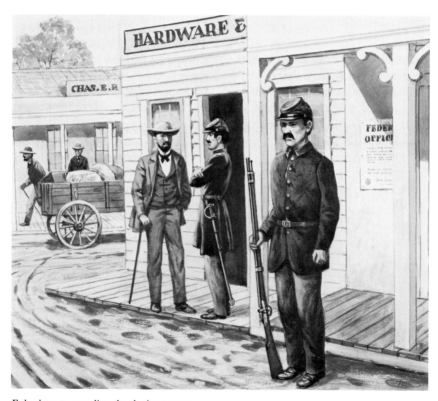

Federal troops guarding the election process

It was during the Reconstruction years that the Silesians began entering the social and political life of the areas in which they lived. Emanuel Rzeppa of Panna Maria initiated this activity by serving as justice of the peace for the precinct encompassing the Polish settlement in 1869, but he was followed by many Silesians in public office. Among these mid-19th century Polish participants in the political process were August Krawietz as constable in Bexar County, Thomas Kiołbassa as city alderman in San Antonio, John Adamietz as both deputy sheriff and county commissioner in Bandera, Albert Adamietz as county treasurer at Bandera, and Alexander Dziuk (the Civil War veteran) as county commissioner, Albert Kasprzyk and P. Jurecki as constables, and Joseph Kyrish, John Gawlik, and John Kusar as members of a committee investigating fire damage to the courthouse, all in Karnes County.

John Adamietz

Hog slaughtering at Falls City, 1921

The Poles Come to East Texas

The social and economic problems which caused so much trouble for the Silesians in the San Antonio area somewhat ironically set the stage for the beginnings of Polish immigration to east Texas, the other major area in the state in which Poles settled. The immediate cause prompting their immigration was the freeing of the Negro slaves upon whom the planters had depended as laborers on their cotton plantations.

A group of Walker County cotton planters met in a general store at Old Waverly, Texas, on September 19, 1866, to discuss their problems in securing workers. At this very time the landowners may have been wondering how to get their 1866 cotton crop out of the fields and to the cotton gins. The store where the men met was owned by Meyer Levy, a Polish Jew who had lived for many years in the South and who had various holdings in the state.

Meyer Levy was himself an interesting person. He departed Europe in 1848, spending a short time in England, and then emigrated to the United States about 1850, landing at Norfolk, Virginia. He worked as a merchant and trader throughout the Southern states in the years before the Civil War and appears to have traded at various points on the Brazos River in Texas as early as 1858. After the outbreak of the conflict Levy reportedly received a letter of marque from the Confederacy and operated as a privateer and blockade runner, trading among Southern ports, England, and the West Indies. His family lived in New Orleans during the war, and his wife, the former Jane Hart of Georgia, is said to have

61

been imprisoned by federal troops after they occupied New Orleans on account of her "impertinence to a Yankee officer." After the Confederate collapse Levy returned to Texas, selling his ship to secure capital in order to reestablish his mercantile business. It was a store built with this money in Old Waverly where the planters met in September 1866.

The minutes of the meeting record the foundations laid for the arrival of the first organized group of Poles in east Texas six months later. The 12 planters gathered there "for the purpose of Considering the propicity [sic] of sending to Europe for foreign laborers." C.T. Traylor was selected as chairman of the meeting, and H.M. Ellmore was appointed secretary. The members established themselves as the Waverly Emigration Society and commissioned Meyer Levy to travel to Europe to recruit 150 "foreign laborers" to work on their lands. Each planter requested a certain number of workers, some of them asking for specific types of skills, such as cook, house servant, "man about the Yard," blacksmith, carpenter, gardener, "one Woman to cook, Wash, Iron & Husk." The planters agreed to pay for the passage of the immigrants to Texas and to pay the men $90, $100, and $110 for their work in their first, second, and third years in America respectively, with women receiving $20 less for their labors each year. In addition, the planters obligated themselves to provide the workers with a "comfortable cabin" and food.

"The First Bale of Cotton," engraving by Frenzeny & Tavernier

The immigrants, in return, were expected "to do faithful labors and all that may be required" as workers "on a Cotton Plantation, in Walker Co., in the State of Texas, . . . for the period of three years, from the date of landing in Texas." In addition, the immigrants were expected to repay to the planters from their salaries in three installments the cost of their passage to America.

As the agent of the Waverly Emigration Society Levy sailed for Europe to recruit the "foreign laborers" for the Walker County plantations. Finding that Polish peasants in the years after the unsuccessful Polish Insurrection of 1863 were eager to emigrate to America, he recruited a party of them and sailed to New York. According to one source, he allowed the emigrants to leave the ship at New York "to see the city" while the vessel was being stocked with the provisions for the remaining trip to Texas, and when the time came to sail "none of them reappeared." He, thus, was forced to return to Europe for another group of emigrants, which he did, arriving with them on the Texas coast sometime in April 1867. The group of peasant farmers passed through Houston in the fourth week of April and then made their way to Walker County, about 60 miles to the north. Thus, in May 1867 the first Polish immigrants to east Texas arrived at their new homes.

The Poles settled in and around what became the town of New Waverly. They soon were joined by other Polish immigrants who had come to Texas on their own and had heard that there already were Poles living in the New Waverly area.

During their initial years in the state the east Texas Poles worked as agricultural laborers for the land owners, but within a decade some of them already were buying their own land and erecting their own homes. As years passed and the lumbering industry grew in the Walker County area, many young men from the Polish settlement worked in the sawmills. This type of employment, as was the case with agricultural labor, gave them the cash money they needed to buy their own farms. By the beginning of this century the New Waverly Poles had bought almost all the farmland near the community and had purchased or were buying considerable amounts of land outside the immediate area.

New Waverly served as the mother colony for most of the Polish colonies later established in east Texas. Although it was located in the Trinity River basin, the other colonies were in the Brazos River valley, most of them in the rich bottomland which was ideal for growing cotton. Large numbers of Poles passed through New Waverly on the way to such communities as Anderson, Brenham, and Chappell Hill.

The story of the Joseph Bartuła family was repeated time after time with only names, places, and dates changed, as hundreds of Polish families came to east Texas. Bartuła was a cartwright from the village of Brzostek, located in Pilzno County in Austrian Poland. He and his wife and five children emigrated to Texas in 1873. They landed at Galveston and journeyed to New Waverly, where they

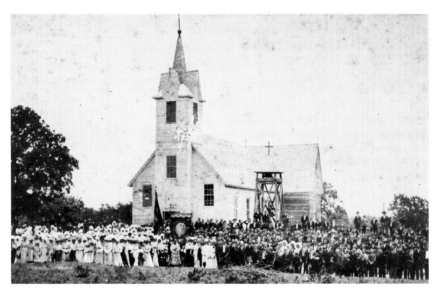

St. Mary's Catholic Church at Bremond, about 1900

St. Joseph's Catholic Church at New Waverly

heard that they would find other Poles. They spent a few months at New Waverly, and then Bartuła decided to move on to Bremond. Living there well into the 20th century, Bartuła was well known in his older years as the founder of what became the major center of Polish population in Robertson County.

In east Texas the Polish Catholic parishes indicate the location of Polish settlements. As early as 1867, for example, the Reverend Felix Orzechowski, a priest serving as a missionary in Texas from the Congregation of the Resurrection, began visiting New Waverly to minister to the religious needs of the Poles living there. After spending several months working under primitive conditions in the Walker County area, he established Saint Joseph's Church at New Waverly in 1870. This was the first Polish church founded in east Texas, and it served as a base of operations for other Polish missionaries in surrounding towns.

From the first years of Polish settlement New Waverly served as a funnel for immigrants to other areas, such as the nearby towns of Plantersville and Anderson. In these two latter locations the Poles followed economic pursuits more or less the same as at New Waverly: they farmed first on rented land and then, after they had saved enough money, bought their own property. From Saint Joseph's parish at New Waverly, Father Orzechowski visited both of these newer colonies, offering Masses in the homes of the immigrants. Six years after the founding of the church at New Waverly, the Poles opened a new church at Anderson, with Plantersville as its mission. Although the original church at Anderson has been replaced, there remains a Polish parish in the town with beautiful stained glass windows portraying Polish saints. Today the Polish parish for the Plantersville community is located in nearby Stoneham. Anderson always has had a greater population than Plantersville, a position which was enhanced when approximately 100 new Polish immigrant families settled there after 1880.

The northernmost of the east Texas Polish colonies was the next to be established. This community, Marlin, has a claim to age almost as great as that of New Waverly. One writer recorded that as early as 1870 "quite a group" of Poles were already living in the town, while one of the early settlers there claimed that in 1880 there were approximately 30 Polish families in the area. Joseph Bartuła of Bremond stated that in 1877 there were already 60 Polish families living in Marlin, but this must have been an exaggeration, for the Polish population of the town had reached this point only in the early 20th century. In spite of the fact that the Marlin area had been occupied by Poles for many years, by the beginning of this century only 13 of the 60 families living there at that time had managed to buy their own farms. The others rented their land or sharecropped.

A Polish parish came into being at Marlin in 1872, when it was established by the Reverend Joseph Mosiewicz. Through the years the Marlin parish retained its Polish identity, as shown by the fact that 71 of the 87 families in the parish in 1936 were of Polish origin. For a few years the Marlin church became

Hauling cotton bales at Brenham early in the 20th century

a mission of the daughter parish it had formed in nearby Bremond, but later it returned to the status of being an independent parish, as it is today.

Probably the next Polish community to be established was at Brenham, the county seat of Washington County. By 1871 small groups of 15 to 20 Polish families annually began coming to the fertile area around Brenham, which already was occupied by Germans and others. The earlier settlers had started planning for the establishment of a Catholic parish, securing the land about 1870. The Poles joined them in founding the actual parish in 1875. With the passage of time and the arrival of more Slavic immigrants, the Poles came to constitute the majority of the parishioners, so that by 1936 they represented 150 families out of the total of about 200 in the Brenham parish.

Poles began settling in the area around Chappell Hill, 10 miles east of Brenham, about the same time that they started settling around the latter. In the rich, black soil of the Chappell Hill area many of the Poles became wealthy farmers. A description of the Chappell Hill-Brenham Poles early this century demonstrates the level of affluence that they had achieved: "It is a pleasant sight to watch the Polish farmers on their way to church . . . in [their] comfortable, even elegant carriages, with expensive harness and handsome, well-cared-for horses."

In the early years priests from Brenham visited Chappell Hill to minister to the settlers there, but in 1889 the Poles in the area decided to organize their own separate parish. It exists to this day as the Saint Stanisław parish of Chappell Hill.

In 1873 the first small parties of Poles began moving to the vicinity around Bryan. They came there either from the existing Polish communities in east Texas or directly from Europe for the next three decades. The Bryan Poles, unlike many of their fellow countrymen in the other Polish colonies, lived in a very mixed society. The town was first occupied by various people, including substantial numbers of Irish settlers, and it grew through the arrival of Poles, Czechs, and Italians. Perhaps because none of these ethnic groups were dominant, relations among them were friendly and conducted in more social areas than in communities in which one group predominated. In the early years all the Catholics in the town shared the same church, with each group having special ethnic services and festivals of their own. Bryan, which actually attempted to recruit new immigrants, advertised itself and its Brazos valley region in brochures which were printed in multiple languages. Several steamship companies had agents' offices in the downtown Bryan business district. Such inducements undoubtedly must have influenced some of the Poles to come to Bryan rather than to settle in other towns or regions.

As already mentioned, Polish settlement at Bremond began with the arrival of the Joseph Bartuła family in 1875. Bartuła found a job on the J.C. Roberts plantation, was satisfied with the conditions he found, and started writing letters to other Poles who then moved to the area. This started the Polish colony at Bremond. Large numbers of Poles came to the area in the next few years, making it probably the largest single concentration of Poles in the state. When Stefan

Nesterowicz, a visiting Polish journalist from the North, came to Bremond in the early 20th century, he declared, concerning the town: "I am in the capital of Texas Polonia."

Despite Nesterowicz's praise everything did not always go easily for the Bremond Poles. When the 50 Polish families there decided to build a church in 1877, they were so impoverished that they could raise only 115 dollars. It was only the assistance of others living in the area that allowed the Bremond Poles to

Stefan Nesterowicz and family

erect their church, and even after it was built they could not afford to pay their first pastor a salary. He was forced by economic necessity to raise cotton as a side occupation to give himself an income.

As the years passed many of the Poles in Bremond became successful merchants and farmers. Six decades after the founding of their ethnic community, a historian of the region gave them credit for having been the principal element in the economic development of Bremond. The Poles came into commercial prominence in the town; they were the largest religious body in the county and, in general, took the commanding position in the social and ethnic affairs of the Poles in east Texas. Stefan Nesterowicz was right: Bremond did become "the capital of Texas Polonia."

Street scene at Bremond, 1907

The later years of the 19th century saw the establishment of three additional Polish colonies in the lower Brazos valley. These communities were within the towns of Bellville, Richmond, and Rosenberg. Many of the Poles who settled in this area came there from the Chappell Hill vicinity.

Working as cotton farmers as they had elsewhere in the state, the Poles in the three southernmost east Texas Polish colonies were slow in founding their own parishes. Even though the Bellville Catholics had erected a church building as early as 1905, it was 1942 before they could support their own resident priest. In the 1930's over half of the 45 Catholic families in the town were of Polish origin. At Richmond it was 1935 before the Catholic parish was organized, although almost 70 years before, land had been secured for the erection of a Catholic church. In 1935, when the church was built, the Catholic congregation

Street scene at Rosenberg, 1912

had 100 families, half of whom were Polish. Rosenberg saw Catholic parochial activities earlier than the other two nearby communities, with a parish founded in 1906, and an initial church built in 1911.

Of all the Polish communities in Texas, Rosenberg was the location of the only Polish National Catholic Church organized in the state. This sect, which stressed the Polish nationality in opposition to what it saw as "Americanization," is not part of the Roman Catholic Church and possesses its separate church hierarchy and clergy. About 40 of the Polish families at Rosenberg left the Catholic church in December 1925 to form their own "Polish National" parish, which met twice monthly for services in the local Presbyterian church building. The group continued to exist until 1938, at which time most of its members returned to the Roman Catholic parish.

Poles have lived in the Houston area for many years. Although Polish individuals have been in the area since the days of Felix Wardzinski and the Texas Revolution, most of the Poles started moving to the city in the 1870's. By the 20th century there were about 200 Polish families in the city, but there never was a separate and distinct Polish Quarter as developed in San Antonio. It was probably this absence of a concentration of Poles in any one area which accounts for the fact that the only Polish organization in the city at the turn of the century was a group of the Polish National Alliance. A Polish Catholic parish was proposed several times, but it never came into existence as such. Despite this situation the Houston Poles found considerable material success in the Bayou City, with one of them telling a visitor in 1909: "There is no place like Houston . . . nowhere is as good as it is in Texas."

Mrs. Felix Urbanczyk and Mrs. Ben Urbanczyk posing with (stuffed) fox

Soldiers from Mexico

One very interesting group of Polish exiles came to Texas in the years following the Civil War. Some of them settled among the Silesians while others located in east Texas. These men were former soldiers in the army of Emperor Maximilian in Mexico.

One of the better known of the exiles was Joseph Sadowski, a native of Grujczyna in Grodno Province of Russian Poland. As a 15-year-old he fought as a sharpshooter in Lelewel's division in the Polish Insurrection of 1863, seeing action at Włodawa and Siemiatycze. After the collapse of the insurrection portions of his division were lured across the border into Austrian Poland by a Polish-speaking Austrian army officer, whereupon they were captured and imprisoned by the Austrians for several months in Kraków and later in Olomouc. After eight months as prisoners this group of former rebels was given the opportunity to leave the prison if its members enrolled in the Austrian army. Sadowski thus joined the Polish Uhlans which within months were sent as part of Maximilian's army to Mexico. His military unit sailed on the English ship *Peru* on a 48-day voyage to Vera Cruz. Fighting for the emperor, Sadowski was captured by the liberals, in whose army he found substantial numbers of Poles who had deserted from the imperial army. Young Sadowski joined them for a while, but then he deserted the liberal cause, "because of the lack of any kind of order." After the death of Emperor Maximilian he received a passport to leave the country, but had no money. "I walked on foot to the coast," he later related, "and having found a ship there, I went on board and was taken, eventually, as a nonpaying guest,

71

Maximilian, emperor of Mexico

Vera Cruz, Mexico, in 1867

to Houston." From there he moved on to Rockport, where he worked for some time in a slaughterhouse, and then about 1880 he settled in Bremond, where he became a farmer.

Another of the exiles from Maximilian's imperial army was Mathew Pilarczyk, who settled in Karnes County. He also came from Europe to Mexico in the army supporting the French-backed Austrian emperor. After Maximilian's fall Pilarczyk was captured by the liberals and, according to the stories he later told, he was due to be killed by a firing squad. "The instant the Mexican gunners started shooting," he related, "one comrade and I broke away and ran. Good fortune attended us while almost all the others were shot down." Pilarczyk continued his tale: "We reached the river and plunged in and swam it with Mexican horsemen on our heels anxious to cut us down." The two men crossed the river and came upon a Mexican teamster hauling wood and offered to give him whatever objects of value they had if he would conceal them. "He saved our lives, for when the horsemen came galloping up asking to be put on the track of fleeing men this teamster directed them away from us and without question saved our lives." Pilarczyk and his friend plodded on day after day until they reached the Rio Grande and safety in Texas. Hearing that there were Poles at Panna Maria, Pilarczyk made his way there, where he settled. In later years he married into one of the Silesian families and became a substantial member of the agricultural community. His grave today lies at the Panna Maria cemetery, and his descendants enjoy telling visitors about their colorful ancestor.

Mr. and Mrs. Mathew Pilarczyk on their 50th wedding anniversary

Polish Life in 19th Century Texas

Most of the Poles who immigrated to Texas, whether to the San Antonio area or to east Texas, had been farmers in the old country. After they arrived in Texas the majority of them continued to till the soil. The fact that most of them continued to live in rural areas and to do the same type of agricultural work to which they had been accustomed in Europe helped to cushion the cultural shock that they felt in immigrating to America.

The Poles in Texas primarily became cotton farmers who raised a few head of livestock on the side. From the outset the immigrants in east Texas grew cotton, and after the Civil War it became the most important crop grown by the Silesians of the San Antonio area. Traditional accounts state that the Silesian Poles learned how to cultivate cotton from freed Negro slaves during the Reconstruction period. As one visiting writer noted, it gave them "the cash that they wanted." Large crops just after the Civil War made substantial profits, but soon the prices plummeted to as low as three cents per pound. An even worse problem followed: the boll weevil invaded Texas cotton fields, destroying thousands of acres of cotton in the fields annually. In Karnes County, where the Poles were almost the only farmers in the 1880's, 44 percent of the 1887 crop was ruined by the insects. Other years were not so bad, however, and 1889 was a good year for the Poles. Some in Karnes County managed to produce a bale of cotton to the acre in addition to making good corn harvests. The next year, the valley of Cibolo Creek in the Silesian settlements was described as "a magnificent picture of great fields of corn & cotton, sorghum, and . . . oats."

A family of cotton pickers

The account described orchards, vineyards, and "great rows of bee stands," adding that "the Emperor of Prussia is not more independent nor near so happy."

Most of the Silesian farmers worked on land that belonged to them or their families, but when the Poles first started moving to east Texas, they worked on land that belonged to other people. The majority of the east Texas Poles simply lacked the money to buy their own land. They used one or the other of two plans to pay the landlords for the use of the land. Some of the Poles agreed to pay a sum of money per acre as rental. Early in this century the amount varied from as little as $2.00 an acre in the New Waverly area to as much as $6.00 an acre in the Chappell Hill vicinity. At some places in the New Waverly area the tenant was allowed to clear brush and trees from a landlord's property and then use the land for farming for a stipulated length of time rent free. Other Polish farmers paid to use land by sharecropping. The farmers received the right to farm the land in exchange for one-fourth of the cotton or one-third of the corn they raised.

According to a report by one agricultural expert, some of the Poles preferred to rent or sharecrop instead of own their land. Like many other frontier farmers, because they did not own the land, they felt no need to fertilize it or attempt to conserve the soil through crop rotation. Thus, by renting, they could make all the profit possible from a piece of ground and then move on to other fields when they had exhausted the nutrients in the soil. Though such procedures may have been profitable to individuals, they clearly were damaging to the future economy of the region.

Mr. and Mrs. Paul Mika and family of Panna Maria

Fortunately most Polish farmers were eager to own their own farms. The desire to possess land, in fact, became a compulsion for some of the immigrants. A Polish observer just after World War I noted that all the American merchants and farmers with whom he had talked who lived around the Poles stressed that the characteristic desire of the immigrants was to buy land. Another Polish visitor a few years earlier noted that the desire to own land was a particularly Polish trait because, through the centuries in Poland, land ownership had been tied to political rights. He reported that nothing could cause the Silesians of the San Antonio area to sell their land, and they always wanted to buy more. He added, "There are peasants [in Texas] whose land is worth 50,000 rubles [$25,000], but who are as poor as when they arrived."

The autobiography of one of the Polish immigrants, Peter Górski, tells about the change from tenancy to land ownership:

> When I came to Marlin in 1880 there were about thirty Polish families that had been living here for some time . . .
>
> Not one of these owned his own land. They paid the landowners three dollars an acre rent, or gave them a third of the corn harvested and a quarter of the cotton.

The Pollok family of Panna Maria, 1913

Mrs. Felix Mika Sr. of Panna Maria, working in her vegetable garden

Twenty years ago [c. 1888], the first to buy land was J. Przybylski. He paid fourteen dollars an acre. Soon after that E. Wilganowski followed in his footsteps and bought a farm.

I farmed on rented land for twenty-two years, and seven years ago [c. 1901] I bought a hundred acres for forty-two fifty an acre, paying cash for the whole.

Today I wouldn't take seven thousand five hundred dollars for the same land.

The Poles in Texas were considered by others to be very good farmers, a reputation which they retain today. Under the same conditions the Poles almost always produced more cotton than others who lived around them. There are a number of factors which contributed to this situation, but one of the most important was that the Poles worked in the fields themselves. Because the Poles owned the land and had immediate benefits from their hard work, they had motivation that hired workers lacked. In addition, entire Polish families worked in the fields with the men at harvest or when more labor was needed. They more than doubled their work force in times of need without requiring any additional financial outlay for labor.

Cooperation was one of the interesting features of Polish agriculture in Texas during the late 19th and early 20th centuries. This cooperation frequently was within families, such as father and sons working together at harvest or haying. Such efforts were quite evident among the three Urbanczyk brothers, Ben, John, and Felix, during the early years at White Deer in the Texas Panhandle. The two younger brothers, Ben and Felix, bought many things together: tractors, land, cattle, and automobiles. They even shared the first well that they drilled —

Ben Urbanczyk astride his threshing machine, 1908

79

located halfway between their two houses. When heavy agricultural machinery became more readily available, the Urbanczyks bought their own wheat-threshing equipment together. At harvest time Ben ran a big Rhumley steam engine, Felix operated the threshing machine, and John supervised the hauling of grain to the threshing area with horses and wagons.

The other form of cooperation common among the Poles was among neighbors, usually in age groups. The men who had grown up and played together as youths helped each other with their agricultural work as older men. This was a general exchange of working time in which, for example, the farmers of a certain area met at one farm to harvest a crop and then moved on to the next farm and then the next until the harvest for them all was completed. As mechanization continued in the 20th century the exchanges among same-age groups were replaced with contract work. As one man bought a corn picker, another purchased a hay baler, etc., and with a comparatively limited capital outlay entire neighborhoods became mechanized.

Felix Urbanczyk and family at White Deer, 1917

Business and Commerce

Although the struggle required great effort on their part, most of the Poles who came to Texas advanced both socially and economically. Some of the immigrants found their success in agriculture, while others did so in business and commerce. One of the most prominent Poles during the 19th century was Edward Kotula, who became an influential merchant in San Antonio. He was born in Silesia in 1844, immigrating to Texas as a boy and living first at Panna Maria and then at San Antonio. His father died while he was a boy, so from an early age Edward had to earn a living for himself. First working as a teamster, he later began carrying mail on horseback between towns during the Civil War. After the conflict he secured a position as a clerk in the mercantile establishment owned by Dan and Anton Oppenheimer in San Antonio. Rapidly moving up in the firm, he then invested his savings in an adobe general store with a capital of 1500 dollars. He succeeded and continued to expand his commercial business until he finally moved his store into a large business located on Military Plaza in the city. Entering other commercial areas, particularly ranching, real estate, and wool marketing, he built a reputation as a "wool king of Texas." After 1893 Kotula closed his store on Military Plaza and devoted his efforts to his other interests. He died in 1907, a greatly respected member of the San Antonio business community.

The range of the economic mobility of the east Texas Poles may be seen in the numbers of commercial establishments they owned. At the beginning of this century in Bremond, the center of the greatest Polish commercial activity, there

Ed Kotula as a student at St. Mary's College in San Antonio, 1888

Advertisement for Ed Kotula & Co.

Interior of Ed Kotula's store on Military Plaza in San Antonio

82

were many Polish-owned businesses: three blacksmiths, two cotton gins, a butcher shop, a wholesale beer distributor, several saloons, several grocery stores, one pharmacy, one dry goods store, and a hotel. In contrast, at the same time the Bryan colony had only one Polish business to patronize, a saloon.

Not all the Poles were successful. One notable Pole who "went bad" was Martin Mróz, a young Silesian from the San Antonio area who became an outlaw in the Pecos River valley of New Mexico and far west Texas. Martin left the San Antonio area in the 1880's and, with three other young Poles, went to Live Oak County to become a cowboy.

Dee Harkey, who later became a United States marshal, was a friend of Mróz at the time, and he later wrote of these days: "I knew him when he couldn't talk English." Mróz moved on west, and by 1890 he had gathered his own band of cattle thieves operating in the Pecos River valley near present-day Carlsbad, New Mexico. He was described as "a big, rough, blue-eyed blond who wore neither underwear nor boots," but who went about in a pair of rough brogan shoes. He married a buxom, fair-haired prostitute in the saloon town of Phoenix, New Mexico, and built up a notorious reputation as a man not to be disagreed with.

In the spring of 1895 the local cattlemen's association offered a reward for the arrest of Mróz. He was captured, then escaped, and finally fled across the border to Juarez. There he was arrested by Mexican authorities but subsequently released from jail. In the meantime his wife had come to El Paso, on the Texas side of the river, to try to get him out of the Mexican jail. She hired the well-known gunman, John Wesley Hardin, who had read law in prison and who had been pardoned by the Texas governor, as her attorney to secure Martin's release from jail in Juarez. After Mróz was freed he was surprised and angered to learn that his wife and Hardin were living together in a rooming house across the river. To add insult to injury, the two were living on money which he had left in his wife's possession. Because of the reward for his arrest, Martin was unable to cross the border for fear of apprehension by lawmen. Finally on June 29, 1895, he was lured across a railway bridge by United States Marshal George Scarborough on the pretext of seeing his wife and was killed. As Dee Harkey recollected, "When Martin and Scarborough started

John Wesley Hardin

83

A street scene in Juarez, Mexico, about the time that Martin Mróz was evading law officers

through the weeds [at the American end of the bridge], I do not know what was said, but Scarborough killed Martin." The body of Mróz was buried in the Concordia Cemetery at El Paso, and within only a few weeks the space next to him was filled by the mortal remains of his rival, John Wesley Hardin, who was killed in a gunfight.

Relations between the Poles and other Texans should not be judged by those of Martin Mróz with the lawmen of El Paso and the Pecos valley. The relations between the two groups, however, must be viewed in two parts: those of the Texans with the Silesians of the San Antonio area and with the east Texas Poles.

After the end of the Reconstruction period the Silesians and their Texas neighbors lived in comparative harmony, although the two groups continued to remain somewhat distant in all but commercial and official dealings.

The Polish settlers were not the only immigrants to suffer discrimination and unfair harassment at the hands of earlier settlers. This is often the case as the people who feel themselves "native" come to fear economic competition or act on social prejudice.

There were occasions when other Texans came to the aid of the Silesians, as one did by giving the stone for the building of a new church at Saint Hedwig in 1867. In another gesture of good feeling toward the Poles, three times more Americans than Poles attended the 1879 funeral of the Reverend Bronislaus Przewłocki at Bandera.

In east Texas the Poles appear to have been considered by some as mere replacements for the black slaves. The separation of the white Southerners and the immigrants was shown by R.L. Daniels in an 1883 article published in *Lippincott's Magazine,* in which an east Texas Polish farmer was portrayed as calling his landlord "Massa," a term generally reserved for use by the former slaves in addressing their masters. Daniels observed that during a Polish wedding feast he attended in east Texas, the doors and windows of the house were filled by spectators who were "mostly our colored friends, who good-naturedly condescend on such occasions to patronize 'dem white niggahs,' whom they hold in undisguised contempt." Only a few sentences farther in the article, he noted the literacy of the Poles, stating that an astonished Negro man remarked, "Dey kin write an' cipher same like *white* folks." Clearly, for many years the east Texas Poles held a somewhat subordinate position.

Relations of the Poles with the Negroes also were mixed. In the Silesian settlements of south Texas the two groups generally got along amicably. After the Civil War it was the freed slaves who reportedly taught the Silesians how to cultivate cotton, and during these years some of the Poles employed blacks as agricultural laborers.

In east Texas the Poles and the blacks were in direct economic competition, a situation which did not provide a background for good relations. Each group, however, seems to have been able to accommodate itself to the presence of the other, and very few examples of conflict between them have been noted. When Stefan Nesterowicz visited the east Texas Polish colonies early in this century, he observed interestingly that the spoken English of the Polish farmers in Plantersville and Anderson was something akin to "the Negro dialect" because "They have more to do with the blacks than with the Americans." Even more curious was the journalist's comment that in the Chappell Hill area, "almost every black understands a few words of Polish," an ability that few whites were able or willing to show.

The principal European ethnic group with whom the Polish Texans had dealings were the Germans. In east Texas there seem to have been comparatively smooth relations, as was the case between the Silesian Poles and the Germans in the San Antonio area. There were exceptions. The earliest known conflict between the two groups was over language use in the Catholic church at Meyersville in DeWitt County. This conflict was resolved when most of the Poles left that parish and joined other Poles in the Yorktown church. After the Civil War the two groups again had a disagreement related to religious matters. In 1866 the Germans in San Antonio were actively organizing their own separate Catholic parish, and they attempted to convince the Poles to join them. Seeing what he felt to be an attempt of the organizers to Germanize the Poles, their pastor, Father Vincent Barzyński,

Reverend Vincent Barzyński, about 1866

Faculty and students of St. Joseph's School, Meyersville, about 1898

The Rafael Kolodziejczyk family of Yorktown

protested: "The Germans are great for giving advice and ruling the Poles . . . but we . . . do not want to change our faith for theirs, because we Poles have our own saints in heaven." The Germans then organized their parish without the help of the Poles.

John Moczygemba and family

Only the Silesian Poles had dealings with Mexicans, but these were of long standing. From their first days in Texas the Silesians had known the Mexicans, initially as the teamsters who drove oxcarts for them from the coast to the sites of their settlements inland. In addition, it was a Mexican, Andreas Coy, who was one of the first persons to help the Poles during the great drought of 1856–57. Soon the relations between the two groups became even more intimate, with one of the Silesians, who happened to be one of the Reverend Moczygemba's brothers, marrying into a Spanish family during the early years of settlement.

Spanish-speaking people frequently lived near the Silesians, and many of the young Poles first learned their native Polish, then Spanish as a second language, and finally English as a third. A visiting Polish anthropologist in 1930 said that the Mexicans had influenced Silesian culture in Texas more than other groups.

One group of nonagricultural Poles in Texas were the coal miners who worked for a number of years at Thurber, about 70 miles west of Fort Worth. The town was the site of mines opened in 1886 by the Johnson Coal Company and sold in 1888 to the Texas and Pacific Coal Company, a subsidiary of the Texas and Pacific Railway. A high percentage of the inhabitants of the company town were immigrants, and most of the actual underground work was done by Poles and Italians, who lived on what was known as Hill Number 3. A railway line leading to the mines bisected the hill, with the Poles living on the south side and the Italians on the north.

Among the best-remembered occasions in Thurber were its Polish weddings. Before the service in the Thurber Catholic Church the bride and groom in their

Downtown Thurber, 1910

July 4th celebration at Thurber, 1910

View of Thurber, town owned by the Texas & Pacific Mining & Mercantile Company

89

Wedding of Pauline Tudyk and Thomas Katzmarek at St. Hedwig, 1894

festive dress were driven about the town to show off their finery. After the wedding service the couple rode to the bride's parents for a magnificent wedding feast. Frequently hundreds of guests attended the celebrations, which sometimes lasted for three and four days. When night came it was time for dancing either in the parents' home or in the dance hall located on "Polander Hill." These dances also served as a means of securing money for the new couple. In order to dance with the bride it was necessary for a man to throw a coin, trying to break a big, thick dinner plate. If he failed to shatter the plate, he lost both his money and his opportunity to dance. Most of the guests chose to throw silver dollars, which were more likely to break the plates. As one historian of Thurber wrote, "It was not uncommon for the newly married couple to receive three or four hundred dollars by the time the celebration was over," adding, "if the bride was pretty and popular, and if she chose her attendants with care, the 'plate breaking' income would often be more."

Most of the Poles left Thurber when the coal mines closed in 1921, although a few remained for a decade to work in the nearby oil field and brick factory. In 1933 the company closed the town entirely, demolished most of the buildings, and left it the ghost town that it remains today.

Mr. and Mrs. Valentine Yanta and daughter Mary of Panna Maria

Polish Texans in the 20th Century

As the years passed the manifestations of the 20th century began appearing in the Polish towns and communities. When a Polish visitor arrived at Falls City in 1907, he looked around from the railway platform to see the wooden false-front buildings and loungers watching the day pass by only to be surprised with the discovery that "there are telephones in this desert!" Not long after this visitor came to Texas, automobiles began appearing in the Polish colonies. One of the first Silesian families to own one was the Valentine Yanta family, who lived on Ecleto Creek in Karnes County and used their Jackson automobile to drive back and forth to church services and activities at Panna Maria.

Not all the Poles accepted the changes that the new century was forcing on the settlements. The new ideas and new things were discomforting to many of the older Poles who had come from Europe and were accustomed to the old way of life. Such a person was Joseph Moczygemba of Panna Maria, one of the brothers of the Reverend Leopold Moczygemba, who had been born in Upper Silesia in 1819. In Poland he was married and the father of five children, when he came to Texas at his brother's suggestion in 1854. Either on the ship or just after arrival in Texas his wife died, leaving Joseph to care for a large family, so he remarried in Texas at the age of 36. He had five more children by his second wife.

Becoming a successful Karnes County farmer, Joseph Moczygemba was active in church and community affairs, but with advancing age he became increasingly infirm and feeble. When he had reached the age of 91 his son plaintively wrote

Mr. and Mrs. Joseph Moczygemba

to relatives in Silesia that the old man's health was so poor that he could no longer recognize his children and that he was losing his ability to speak. Sadly the son wrote: "Mother is afraid that he will go mad because he is thinking about the old country, about his Fathers, even though they've been lying in their graves for a long time . . . he is sitting and thinking day and night . . . and desires death."

One of the major events of the new century that touched all of the Poles in the state was the First World War. On the home front probably the most important effect of the conflict was the temporary prosperity that it brought to the Polish farmers in the rural areas. High wartime prices for agricultural products gave them more spending money than many of them could remember ever having. One Pole recalled from his childhood during the war that, although products like white sugar and flour were obtainable only in restricted amounts, "nice new cars were in vogue," and often in the Polish settlements it seemed that "many a farmer wallowed in money."

The world war began for the Polish Texans in 1917, when the United States declared war on the Central Powers. During the years when men were evading conscription in other parts of the country, the Polish districts had high volunteer rates. Large numbers of Texas Poles went abroad, like Władysław Zaiontz, who fought the Germans on the western front, Adolf Kiołbassa who fought in several battles with the American Expeditionary Forces, and Onufry Zaiontz who served in the Meuse region and in the Argonne Forest.

Just a few years after the war an observer noted that "on the walls of many a quiet farm home . . . hang pictures of big, shy Polish boys in American khaki and trench cap. And in some homes the picture is all they have left of the boy."

Despite the fact that men from Texas with names like Baranowski, Moczygemba, Jankowski, Murski, and Gutowski gave their lives for their country, the years immediately following the war were filled with discrimination against the Poles. These were the years when the Ku Klux Klan and other nativist organizations campaigned against virtually everything that they identified as non-American, particularly if they were foreign or Roman Catholic. The Poles met both of these criteria.

In Karnes County the situation in the early 1920's became so severe that many families at Panna Maria were afraid to travel the short distance to nearby Karnes City for fear of verbal and physical abuse. One of the Silesians recalled that when he went to town as a boy he was "sort of pushed around and laughed at" by the Americans who made fun of him as "a damned Polander and a God-damned Catholic." At White Deer, where the Poles were especially visible as they were virtually the only ethnic minority, the discrimination was severe. The Polish children at a public school had almost daily fights with the other children, who imitated their parents in calling the newcomers "Polocks and damn Catholics." Since they could barely understand English the Polish children surely could not comprehend why the other children mistreated them.

Probably the greatest show of antiforeign feeling directed against the Poles took place at Brenham. On the night of May 18, 1921, about 500 white-robed,

Theatrical performance at the Catholic Church in Brenham, 1930

torch-bearing members of the Ku Klux Klan arrived in town by chartered train from Houston and staged an antiforeign parade through the principal commercial streets. In their high-pointed white caps, white flowing robes, and white face masks, the Klansmen marched behind a robed horseman and two color guards carrying a large American flag. Several of the parading Klansmen carried large placards with messages including "Speak English or quit talking on Brenham's streets" and "Get it right, an American is one who is for his country and against the world."

Following the Klan parade, the situation became so heated in the Brenham area that people from the country stopped coming to town to trade and reportedly were afraid to leave their homes to go to church. In hopes of at least discussing the problems, the most prominent citizens of the town met in the district courtroom for the purpose of finding some means of returning to stability. The session, among other actions, passed these three resolutions which remained in effect for the next few months:

1. Funeral services for soldiers must be in English.
2. Business transactions must be in English.
3. Ministers must preach in English.

In time the severe difficulties between the Poles and the Klan subsided, but the bad feelings remained for many years. It is not possible today to measure the psychological damage which may have been caused, especially to the children, but the fear and hurt they felt may provide an explanation why most Poles in the state prefer to stress their friendship with the Americans and not talk about the times they would prefer to forget.

The economic prosperity that the Polish farmers in Texas experienced during World War I soon passed. With the 1920's came the agricultural depression which preceded by almost a decade the general economic depression of the 1930's. The fact that many of the Polish farmers had diversified farms, raising not only cash crops but also feed grains, gardens, and livestock, allowed many of them to survive the economic hardships of the depression. One Pole at White Deer recollected: "The depression was pretty bad, but a farmer never starves if he works. You got your chickens, your eggs, a pig or two . . . There is nothing to buy but a little flour and coffee." The difficulties of raising cash crops were illustrated by an incident in which a visiting Pole from the Northern states came upon a farmer with a three-horse team plowing under a beautiful crop of onions between the Kosciuszko and Czestochowa colonies in 1936. Upon being asked why he was destroying the crop, the bitter Polish farmer replied that the price of onions was less than ten cents a bushel and that he preferred to plow under the crop than sell it at such a low price.

Many of the Poles in the state sought escape from the economic problems of the depression. Some of them found this release by following the activities of

"Tractored Out," a Texas farm scene photographed in 1938 by Dorothea Lange

one of their own, Fabian Kowalik, called the "Mayor of Falls City." He was a well-known pitcher for the Chicago Cubs baseball team in the mid-1930's, and his participation with the team was followed closely by the "home folks." They were especially excited when Kowalik played in the 1935 World Series.

Other Poles sought a more concrete escape from their economic problems. Some of these people left the older Polish colonies entirely and founded a new settlement in Hidalgo County in the Lower Rio Grande Valley of Texas. Locating around McCook, they slowly built up a Polish community which by 1936 had 20 families and by 1950 had enough Poles for the establishment of its own separate Catholic church.

The Second World War came to the Polish Texans when the Japanese attacked Pearl Harbor in 1941. After the American

Fabian Kowalik

98

declaration of war the Poles in the state were able to come to the assistance of both their Polish motherland and their American homeland. A great many of the men and women had opportunities to prove their bravery. Among them, typically, was Gervase A. Gabrysch of Falls City, who served on a submarine chaser in the Pacific which was sunk by the Japanese. Gabrysch escaped to Australia and continued fighting.

Since the Second World War there have been advances and losses in terms of Polish culture in the state. Although the use of the Polish language continues to decrease, numerous organizations promote the preservation of ethnic culture. Older associations such as the Polish Roman Catholic Union and the Polish National Alliance maintain active chapters in many of the communities, while newer bodies such as the Polish American Congress of Texas, the Polish Arts and Culture Foundation, and the Polish American Priests Association have arisen in the last decade to promote Polish ethnic affairs in their own individual ways. In San Antonio the Polish American Center and in Houston the Polish Home, each with long years as centers of Polish culture, continue actively as centers of ethnic life.

A meeting of the Polish National Alliance at Bremond, 1899

Recent major events for the Poles in the state have been large celebrations. One of these was the 1954 centennial of the founding of the Panna Maria colony, which several thousand visitors attended and which included a field Mass concelebrated by a number of priests, sermons in both English and Polish, music from a men's choir combined from several parishes, and an all-day barbecue dinner. Eclipsing the 1954 celebration a dozen years later was the commemoration of the millennium of Polish Christianity, observed at Panna Maria in 1966. The event included the official dedication of a beautiful mosaic of the Virgin of Częstochowa which President Lyndon B. Johnson gave to the settlement in honor

The White House ceremony commemorating 1,000 years of Christianity in Poland

of its being the oldest Polish colony in America. Other activities included an outdoor Mass and barbecue meal, both of which had become standard for such large Polish celebrations. Also in 1966, as part of the Polish millennium observances, a large grotto was erected in honor of the Virgin of Częstochowa in San Antonio at 138 Beethoven Street, and it remains a place visited by almost all Poles who come to the Alamo City.

Probably the most important undertaking by the Poles in Texas in recent years was the reinterment of the mortal remains of Father Leopold Moczygemba at Panna Maria in 1974. When the pastor from the rural community traveled to Detroit on a pilgrimage to the grave of the founder of the colony, not one of the Polish American clergymen or laymen there was able or willing to take him to the grave of the founder of his parish. Outraged at what they saw as the lack of recognition afforded the priest who founded their community, the oldest Polish

*Shrine of the Virgin of Częstochowa,
patron of Poland*

*Memorial at the grave of the Rev.
Leopold Moczygemba at Panna Maria*

101

Catholic parish in the United States, the people of Panna Maria together with Poles from all parts of the state initiated efforts to have Father Leopold's remains transferred to Texas. They secured the permission of all identifiable next of kin and secured approval from religious and secular officials for the unusual exhumation and reburial. On October 13, 1974, in a large ceremony attended by several thousand visitors and over a dozen priests, two of them from Father Moczygemba's home region in Poland, his body was reinterred at Panna Maria under the same live oak tree beneath which he had offered Christmas Mass for the first Polish colonists in December 1854.

The future of the Poles in Texas is mixed. It is certain that for the foreseeable years Poles will continue to till the soil in the areas where they settled. Their communities will remain islands of Slavic culture in an ocean of American, Mexican, Negro, and other European cultures. The possibility exists for industrialization in the general areas of the Polish settlements, although its prospects are probably greater in Houston, San Antonio, or along the Gulf Coastal Plain. Consequently farming will remain the principal economic activity in the rural areas where the folk culture remains the strongest.

Even today one may walk into country taverns in Polish areas of the state to find only Polish being spoken. There are still well-attended Polish-language Masses in some churches. With the growth of families, however, most of the children go to cities like San Antonio and Houston for employment and higher education, leaving behind only some of their brothers and sisters to maintain the old family farms and to keep up the ethnic culture in the old way. In the cities, where exposure to "American" culture is much greater, the only hope for the retention of the ethnic culture is through participation in Polish religious and secular organizations, where indeed it continues to be preserved.

*A Polish-language grave marker
in the Panna Maria cemetery*

102

Suggested Reading

Bakanowski, Adolf. *Polish Circuit Rider.* Translated and edited by Marion Moore Coleman. Cheshire, Connecticut: Cherry Hill Books, 1971.

A translation to English of portions of the published memoirs of Father Adolf Bakanowski which deal with his years as pastor at Panna Maria, Texas, from 1866 to 1870. Parts of this translation were printed earlier as Adolf Bakanowski, "My Memoirs — Texas Sojourn (1866-70)," translated and edited by Marion Moore Coleman, *Polish American Studies,* 25 (July–December 1968), pp. 106-124.

Baker, T. Lindsay. *The Early History of Panna Maria, Texas.* Texas Tech University Graduate Studies, no. 9. Lubbock: Texas Tech Press, 1975.

The history of the early years of Panna Maria, Texas, founded in 1854, the oldest Polish settlement in the United States.

_____. "The Early Years of Rev. Wincenty Barzyński." *Polish American Studies,* 32 (Spring 1975), pp. 29-52.

Biography covering the early life of the Reverend Vincent Barzyński, including his years in Texas from 1866 to 1874. The article contains historical material concerning the Poles in San Antonio, Saint Hedwig, and Panna Maria, Texas.

_____. *The First Polish Americans: Silesian Settlements in Texas.* College Station: Texas A&M University Press, 1979.

An overall history of all the Silesian Polish settlements in Texas based on both European and American source materials, the majority of them archival sources, but primarily written for general readers.

_____, translator and editor. "Four Letters from Texas to Poland in 1855." *Southwestern Historical Quarterly,* 77 (January 1974), pp. 281-289.

A translation into English of four Polish immigrant letters written from Texas to friends and relatives in Poland in 1855.

_____. "The Moczygemba Family of Texas and Poland: Initiators of Polish Colonization in America." *Stirpes; Texas State Genealogical Society Quarterly,* 15 (December 1975), pp. 124-138.

A detailed account of the history of one of the most prominent pioneer Polish immigrant families in Texas.

_____. "Panna Maria and Płużnica: A Study in Comparative Folk Culture." In *The Folklore of Texan Cultures,* edited by Francis Edward Abernethy, pp. 218-226. Publications of the Texas Folklore Society, 38. Austin: Encino Press, 1974.

A comparative study of the folk culture at the Panna Maria Polish colony in Texas with that of one of the villages in Upper Silesia from which its founders came in the 1850's.

_____. "Silesian Polish Folk Architecture in Texas." In *Built in Texas,* edited by Francis Edward Abernethy, pp. 130-135. Publications of the Texas Folklore Society, 40. Waco: E-Heart Press, 1979.

Brożek, Andrzej. "The Roots of Polish Migration to Texas." *Polish American Studies,* 30 (Spring 1973), pp. 20-35.

The earliest study in the English language to examine the causes of Silesian Polish immigration to Texas.

_____. *Slazacy w Teksasie: Relacje o najstarszych polskich osadach w Stanach Zjednoczonych [Silesians in Texas: Accounts of the Oldest Polish Settlements in the United States].* Warsaw, Poland: Państwowe Wydawnictwo Naukowe, 1972.

Available only in the Polish language, this is the most comprehensive published collection of original source materials on the Silesian Poles in Texas.

Crocchiola, Stanley Francis Louis [F. Stanley]. *The White Deer Texas Story.* Nazareth, Texas: privately printed, 1974.

A booklet-sized general history of White Deer, Texas, containing considerable data on the local Polish community.

Dworaczyk, Edward J. *Church Records of Panna Maria, Texas.* Chicago: Polish Roman Catholic Union of America, 1945.

A translation into English of the baptismal and marriage records of Saint Mary's Church, Panna Maria, Texas, from 1855 to 1863.

_____. *The First Polish Colonies of America in Texas.* San Antonio: The Naylor Company, 1936.

For many years the standard history of the Poles in Texas, this work was written on the occasion of the Texas Centennial in 1936 by the pastor at Panna Maria. It has been reprinted in abridged editions as *The Centennial History of Panna Maria, Texas* in 1954 and as *The Millennium History of Panna Maria, Texas* in 1966, as well as in a full facsimile edition under its original title in 1969.

Haiman, Miecislaus. *The Poles in the Early History of Texas.* Chicago: Polish Roman Catholic Union Archive and Museum, 1936.

The best source of information on individual Polish immigrants to Texas in the first half of the 19th century.

Hodges, LeRoy. "The Poles of Texas: Their Effect on the State's Agricultural Development." *Texas Magazine,* 7 (December 1912), pp. 116-120.

An early published American account of the Poles in Texas, emphasizing their work as farmers.

Hunter, J. Marvin. *A Brief History of Bandera County.* Bandera: Frontier Times, 1936.

A general history of Bandera County, Texas, with valuable information on the Polish immigrants who settled there in 1855.

_____. "When the Polish People Came to Bandera." *Frontier Times,* 25 (May 1948), pp. 191-195.

An account of the founding and early years of Polish settlement at Bandera based on the recollections of one of the actual immigrants.

Iwicki, John. *The First One Hundred Years: A Study of the Apostolate of the Congregation of the Resurrection in the United States 1866-1966.* Rome: Gregorian University Press, 1966.

A history of the activities of the Congregation of the Resurrection in America, based primarily on materials in the archives of the order, containing considerable information on its missions among the Poles in Texas from 1866 to 1895.

Nesterowicz, Stefan. *Travel Notes*. Translated and edited by Marion Moore Coleman. Cheshire, Connecticut: Cherry Hill Books, 1970.

> One of the basic sources on the Poles in Texas during the early 20th century. This book, now available in English translation, was written by a Polish journalist who traveled through the state writing articles for a Polish American newspaper in Toledo, Ohio, which later were compiled into a book.

Przygoda, Jacek. "New Light on the Poles in Texas." *Polish American Studies,* 27 (Spring-Autumn 1970), pp. 80-86.

> An article presenting the results of the author's research on several aspects of Polish Texan history.

——————————. *Texas Pioneers from Poland: A Study in the Ethnic History.* Waco: Privately printed, 1971.

> A general history of the Poles in Texas, examining their activities in all parts of the state.

Randel, Jo Stewart, and Carson County Historical Survey Committee, editors. *A Time to Purpose: A Chronicle of Carson County.* 2 vols. [Seagraves, Texas?]: Pioneer Publishers, 1966.

> A two-volume history of Carson County, Texas, including extensive information on the Polish colony at White Deer.

Starczewska, Maria. "The Historical Geography of the Oldest Polish Settlement in the United States." *The Polish Review,* 12 (Spring 1967), pp. 11-40.

> An unusually fine examination of the historical geography of the Panna Maria settlement, the oldest Polish colony in the United States.

Photo Credits

All prints are from the collections of The University of Texas Institute of Texan Cultures—San Antonio, courtesy of the following lenders. Credits from left to right are separated by semicolons and from top to bottom by dashes.

Page 2 The Institute of Texan Cultures.

Page 3 Manuscript collection of Tulane University Library, New Orleans.

Page 4 San Jacinto Museum of History, Deer Park.

Page 5 General Land Office, Austin.

Page 6 Capitol Building, Austin—Pearl C. Jackson, *Austin: Yesterday & Today* (Austin: American National Bank, 1915).

Page 7 *San Antonio Express,* September 14, 1940.

Page 8 T. Lindsay Baker, Lubbock.

Page 10 Polish Institute of Arts and Sciences, New York City.

Page 11 T. Lindsay Baker, Lubbock.

Page 12 Mrs. A.B. Stephens and Mrs. L.T. Botto, San Antonio.

Page 13 Mrs. Mary B. Stanush, San Antonio.

Page 14 T. Lindsay Baker, Lubbock.

Page 16 Polish American Crusaders Museum, San Antonio; Mr. and Mrs. Rudolph R. San Miguel, San Antonio.

Page 17 Henry H. Brownell, *Pioneer Heroes of the New World* (Cincinnati: Mark R. Barnitz, 1856), page 568—The University of Texas Archives, Austin.

Page 19 Library of the Daughters of the Republic of Texas at the Alamo, San Antonio—*Harper's Weekly,* April 9, 1870, page 236.

Page 21 Mrs. William Ochse, San Antonio—*Gleason's Pictorial Drawing Room Companion.*

Page 22 Frontier Times Museum, Bandera; Mr. and Mrs. Felix Rakowitz, Converse.

Page 24 T. Lindsay Baker, Lubbock—T. Lindsay Baker.

Page 26 Witte Memorial Museum, San Antonio; T. Lindsay Baker, Lubbock—T. Lindsay Baker.

Page 27 T. Lindsay Baker, Lubbock.

Page 29 Albert Kretschmer, *Die Trachten der Völker* (Leipzig, 1906); T. Lindsay Baker, Lubbock.

Page 30 *Harper's Weekly,* May 2, 1868, page 281.

Page 31 Archives, Congregation of the Resurrection, Rome, Italy.

Page 33 Catholic Archdiocese of San Antonio.

Page 34 Mrs. Coy Ross and St. Stanislaus Museum, Bandera—Catholic Archdiocese of San Antonio.

Page 35 Mrs. A.B. Stephens and Mrs. L.T. Botto, San Antonio—*Harper's New Monthly Magazine,* vol. 55, page 833.

Page 36 Panna Maria Museum, Panna Maria.

Page 37 Mr. and Mrs. Rudolph R. San Miguel, San Antonio; Mr. and Mrs. Rudolph R. San Miguel.

Page 40 Mrs. Eleanor Becham, Yorktown.

Page 41 Reverend Peter Kolton, San Antonio.

Page 42 T. Lindsay Baker, Lubbock—T. Lindsay Baker.

Page 43 B.J. Lossing, *Pictorial Field Book of the Revolution* (New York: Harper Brothers, 1859) vol. I, page 49—Mr. and Mrs. Ray Pollok, Falls City.

Page 44 Square House Museum, Panhandle; Square House Museum.

Page 46 Square House Museum, Panhandle.

Page 48 *Atlas to Accompany the Official Records of the Union and Confederate Armies, 1861-1865.*

Page 49 W.H. Emory, "House of Representatives Report on the United States-Mexican Boundary" (Washington, D.C.: Government Printing Office, 1857), vol. I, page 60.

Page 50 *Polish Past in America, 1608-1865* (Chicago, 1939); Mr. and Mrs. Rudolph R. San Miguel, San Antonio.

Page 51 Lewis S. Moat, *Frank Leslie's Illustrated History of the Civil War* (New York, 1895), page 340.

Page 52 The Institute of Texan Cultures.

Page 54 John Cotulla, Cotulla.

Page 56 John F. Dzuik, Hobson.

Page 57 T. Lindsay Baker, Lubbock.

Page 58 Hendrick-Long Publishing Company, Dallas.

Page 59 Mrs. Rosemary Clark, Bandera.

Page 60 Mr. and Mrs. Ray Pollok, Falls City.

Page 62 *Harper's Weekly,* August 21, 1875, page 676.

Page 64 Joe Kotch Sr., Bremond—The Institute of Texan Cultures.

Page 66 John Kaminski, Houston.

Page 67 Stephan Nesterowicz, *Travel Notes: A Translation of Notatkiz podrozy, Toledo, 1909* (Chesire, Conn.: Cherry Hill Books, 1970), page 40.

Page 68 Joe Kotch Sr., Bremond.

Page 69 John A. Speckels Estate, San Antonio.

Page 70 Texas State Archives, Austin.

Page 72 *Harper's Weekly,* April 23, 1864, page 269 — *Harper's Weekly,* August 10, 1867, page 500.

Page 73 Mrs. Ben J. Lyssy, Karnes City.

Page 76 Library of Congress, Washington, D.C.

Page 77 Mr. and Mrs. Felix Snoga, Panna Maria.

Page 78 Mrs. John Yanta, Runge — The Institute of Texan Cultures.

Page 79 Square House Museum, Panhandle.

Page 80 Square House Museum, Panhandle.

Page 82 Mrs. A.B. Stephens and Mrs. L.T. Botto, San Antonio — The Institute of Texan Cultures — Ted Deming, San Antonio.

Page 83 Western History Collection, University of Oklahoma Library, Norman.

Page 85 *Souvenir of El Paso, Texas and Paso del Norte, Mexico* (Columbus, Ohio: Ward Brothers, 1887).

Page 86 Archives, Congregation of the Resurrection, Rome, Italy.

Page 87 Mrs. Doris Fischer Obsta, Victoria; Mrs. Doris Fischer Obsta.

Page 88 Mr. and Mrs. Rudolph R. San Miguel, San Antonio.

Page 89 Joe Martin, Sinton — Joe Martin — Joe Martin.

Page 91 Mr. and Mrs. Emil Mikolayczk, Adkins.

Page 92 Mrs. John Yanta, Runge.

Page 94 John F. Dzuik, Hobson.

Page 95 Sister Jan Maria Wozniak, Providence High School, San Antonio.

Page 98 Library of Congress, Washington, D.C. — The *San Antonio Light* Collection at The Institute of Texan Cultures.

Page 99 Joe Kotch Sr., Bremond.

Page 100 Panna Maria Historical Association, Panna Maria.

Page 101 T. Lindsay Baker, Lubbock — T. Lindsay Baker.

Page 102 T. Lindsay Baker, Lubbock.

Cover The Institute of Texan Cultures.

Index

111